Broken Boundaries

Stories of betrayal in relationships of care

By Sarah Richardson, Melanie Cunningham et al

First published 2008 by WITNESS

Cover design by Syndicut
Cover photo of Sarah Richardson by Catherine Breakspear at Syndicut

Copyright © 2008 WITNESS 32-36 Loman St London SE1 0EH

ISBN 978-0-9558520-0-8

"It is very tempting to take the side of the perpetrator. All the perpetrator asks is that the bystander do nothing. He appeals to the universal desire to see, hear and speak no evil. The victim, on the contrary, asks the bystander to share the burden of pain. The victim demands action, engagement and remembering."

Judith L. Herman

Broken Boundaries

Stories of betrayal in relationships of care

By Sarah Richardson, Melanie Cunningham et al

Broken Boundaries is a collection of seven real-life stories told by the women who have lived them. Each of these women placed their trust in a professional (mental health nurse, psychiatrist, psychotherapist, psychotherapist, mental health social worker, counsellor, GP) at a time of need and vulnerability and each of the professionals exploited that trust. Some of the exploitation was sexual and some was psychological or emotional. All of the exploitation had devastating effects on the women. As a part of their ongoing recovery from the abuse they suffered, each of the women has had the courage and resolve to share their stories. Like so many victims of professional abuse, the women in these stories are highly motivated by the desire to prevent other people being exploited and for those who have, to feel less alone. Each of the authors takes the reader through a telling journey of blurred boundaries, dependency, exploitation and the aftermath.

These stories contain crucial insights for other people going through similar experiences, for those trying to help them and for those who hold positions of trust.

Endorsements

This book of powerful and moving first person accounts brings home to healthcare professionals the importance of boundaries. They exist for a reason: to protect vulnerable patients, and there is never any excuse for crossing them. To do so is an abuse of power, whatever the motivation of the professional. These accounts graphically illustrate the damaging effect that boundary violations have on vulnerable individuals and should be essential reading for any health or social care professional working with such people, and for those involved in professional misconduct cases where a boundary violation is one of the charges.
Moi Ali, Lay Member, Nursing & Midwifery Council

I cannot think of many books that demonstrate as clearly how easy it is for a client to fall under the thrall of a therapist and how easily that power can be misused by an unscrupulous, unboundaried or inexperienced therapist or one lacking in self-awareness or awareness of the responsibility such power carries. I would recommend this book to any client or prospective client who is concerned about their own self-protection and to any therapist/counsellor or trainee who seeks to understand better the dynamics of transference and dependency in the therapeutic relationship and why it is essential that it is anticipated and managed safely.
Yvonne Bates, Author 'Shouldn't I be Feeling Better by Now?'

Immensely valuable in illustrating the levels of inherent trust we all hold in professionals that oath to do no harm. Broken Boundaries' survivors artfully and captivatingly accomplish the emotionally difficult task of detailing the subtle preying on their vulnerabilities by trusted, helping professionals. These brave survivors rose above the even more harmful re-victimization that occurs when reporting to regulatory boards and the lengths exposed offending professionals will go to protect their licenses – at the emotionally harmful expense of their patient.
Cindy Boling, President, Advocate Web

There is a growing interest in increasing access to talking treatments. We know that they have a strong evidence base, are valued by users, and can have extremely positive outcomes. Following increased investment from government, it is likely that many more people will have the chance to benefit. However, with increased availability comes increased risk. Training, supervision, and regulation all play a vital role in ensuring that the experience of service users is a positive one. This book should act as a wake up call to all of us. With searing honesty, it describes the

consequences of broken boundaries and the lack of sufficient supervision. It also shows us the approaches needed to minimise these risks. As access to therapy grows in the UK, we need to make sure we learn all the lessons from other systems.
Paul Farmer, Chief Executive, Mind

As a nurse I know that the vast majority of health and social care professionals are dedicated to caring for their patients/clients but it is a sad fact that there are some who will use their position to abuse patients emotionally, physically and sexually and these cases, along with the many others dealt with by WITNESS, are testimony to that fact. This book highlights just some of the suffering caused to patients/clients when a health care professional blurs or crosses the boundaries be it deliberately or accidentally. Reading these stories brings back memories of my own experience of having been sexually abused by a Psychiatrist, William Kerr, at a time in my life when I was at my most vulnerable. It also reminds me of listening to many of the other ladies who were abused by Kerr and Haslam as they relived not only the actual abuse but more often the after affects which lasted for many more years.
Kathy Haq RGN, Spokesperson for Kerr/Haslam Group

Mainstream therapy introduced universal ethical rules in the 1990s but we still need reminding why clients remain vulnerable and ALL therapists need supervising. This book makes an open and shut case.
Phillip Hodson, Psychotherapist and Broadcaster

An immensely readable, sad and frightening collection of stories from clients in the "care" - but more like abuse - of a variety of dodgy professionals. I really recommend this moving book to anyone who has suffered abuse at the hands of those who they have turned to for professional help.
Virginia Ironside, Author and Agony Aunt

Therapeutic betrayal is devastating. It exploits someone when they are vulnerable and makes the individual doubt their experience, compounding their vulnerability in ways which are unforgivable. Witness speaks up for those whose hurt has been compounded by unscrupulous practitioners who damage. They - the doubly hurt - need robust defending and publishing these stories is a step towards validating individual survivors experiences and to raise awareness of the devastating effects of therapeutic malpractice.
Susie Orbach, Psychotherapist and Author

Endorsements

These courageous and compelling accounts of sexual and emotional abuse by health professionals illustrate victims' pain, suffering and repeated losses. The professionals' callous self-interest and complete absence of care and compassion is astounding. The book will help victims transcend their shame and self-blame, and help families, friends and colleagues avoid re-victimising the sufferer. It should be required reading for student health professionals and those who serve on disciplinary bodies.

P Susan Penfold MB, FRCPC Professor Emeritus, Department of Psychiatry, University of British Columbia, Canada, Author 'Sexual abuse by health professionals: a personal search for meaning and healing'

This book makes difficult painful reading. Women hoping for professional help at a vulnerable time suffered emotional and/or sexual abuse instead. Such violations come from every kind of therapist and professional and pose a continuum of complex legal, ethical and clinical issues. Freud's understanding that the sexual transference was something to work through and not act out is sadly needed just as much now as 100 years ago. This book highlights the need for ongoing training and supervision in understanding traumatic enactments as well as the crucial importance of WITNESS in offering hope to the most vulnerable.

Dr Valerie Sinason, Ph.D.MACP, M.Inst.Psychoanal.

This collection of survivor stories reveals both the incredible strength of the authors and how broad the range of professional exploitation is. The foreword by Gary Schoener discusses aspects of the helping relationship that are manipulated and violated during abuse by helping professionals. In the text, a thread of commonality stitches together these diverse individual accounts of professional abuse, creating a quilt of experiences that covers almost anyone who has ever been exploited, is currently being exploited, or is hovering on the brink of succumbing to a professional abuser. These are raw, visceral stories that shout out the pain, shame, rage, fear, and vulnerability associated with this type of abuse. Although legal recourse is not sought in all of the accounts, another common thread is empowerment from choosing to proceed legally; also, several of the authors subsequently joined helping professions which is also empowering. Sarah Richardson stresses the value of intuition - relearning to listen to one's intuition is key in recovery. Forms of empowerment and healing help to define a border (a boundary, if you will) around the quilt and allow it to have a beginning and an end and eventually be folded and put away. In some fashion, most of these authors, although they will never forget, have moved beyond their abuse. Writing their stories is cleansing and healing and has the added benefit of helping others and, hopefully, preventing future professional exploitation. This is a book from which many will benefit.

Grace Tower, Author *'Fish in a Barrel: A True Story of Sexual Abuse in Therapy'*

The case examples provide insight into the vulnerability of clients in care. If you want to contribute to make professional-client relationships more secure, then recommend this book to read!

Werner Tschan MD, Zurich University Switzerland, President, Association of European Threat Assessment Professionals

Dedication

This book is dedicated to Lynn Hiltz, without whom WITNESS would long ago have bitten the dust.

Acknowledgements and Note to Readers

WITNESS would like to thank the seven women who have shared their stories. We thank them for having the courage to come forward, the fortitude to put their stories down on paper and the generosity to share them with the public. We are certain that these stories will play an important part in helping someone who has been affected by an abusive professional to feel less alone. We also hope that they will educate professionals on the vital importance of safe boundaries and the harm that can be caused if they do not manage these boundaries properly.

We would also like to thank Lorraine Milliard for her skill and warmth much in evidence for the workshop that helped to create this book. Thanks also to Carlie Lee of Pen Friends UK for a superlative professional editing service. And finally, WITNESS would like to thank Awards for All for the grant, without which this would not have been possible.

Sarah Richardson and Melanie Cunningham are real names. All other authors have used noms de plume and other names have been changed except where they are a matter of public record.

Contents

Preface

This book aims to raise awareness of the emotional and sexual exploitation of adults by other adults who occupy positions of authority. Until recently enquiry in this field has been constrained by a high degree of denial on the part of professional groups, by lack of awareness on the part of government and by the needs of the public to maintain trust in those who are trained to help us. We are slowly seeing this situation change. Over the last twenty years awareness of the abuse of children has increased dramatically. More recently we have seen a greater awareness of the abuse of older people. What we are yet to see publically is acknowledgement that people of working age are also subject to exploitation by people in positions of authority.

It is often very difficult for victims and survivors to speak out and, tellingly, only two of the seven contributors, Sarah Richardson and Melanie Cunningham, have felt able to be identified by their real names, the others choosing noms de plume. It is not uncommon to talk about how the feelings of shame and guilt experienced by so many victims of abuse can be serious obstacles to disclosure. What is less often discussed is stigma. Stigmatising people who have been victimised by people in positions of authority is an unacknowledged phenomenon, often underpinning and slanting investigations, court action and mainstream responses to the health and social needs of victims. In part this stems from a view that 'this couldn't happen to me' or 'I would never let this happen to me'. This quasi-magical thinking is no different to the fantasy that we alone will survive the plane crash or be the one who knows how to move in time to avoid the lift fall. These distancing mechanisms can mean the difference between justice and its absence, leaving victims further marginalised even as those who brought about their pain go unpunished.

Another major obstacle to justice, repeatedly confirmed by abuse inquiries, is that when victims decide to report abuse their stories are often not believed. Professional groups sometimes appear to believe that taking the victim's story seriously and confirming that what they describe constitutes abuse is in some way a final arbitration, which may only be determined in a conduct panel hearing. The thinking appears to be that (professional) authority alone determines truth and alone will decide on what is and is not appropriate terminology.

The truth is that making a report about an abusive professional takes courage, strength and determination. It may involve discussing extremely personal and upsetting events, which may not have been disclosed before, even to loved ones; it may mean having these experiences questioned and one's integrity and honesty challenged. Defendants may seek to pathologise or blame victims, describe them as 'personality disordered', deny their experience, even lie on oath. In some cases defendants have intimidated and harassed people, including false reports to the police, threatening phone calls and counter allegations of abuse.

It is in this context that most people (up to ninety percent) choose not to take any formal action. What does this tell us about how widespread these occurrences might really be?

Often prevention of abuse programmes have focused on signs and symptoms (bruising, behaviour changes etc) and on educating about policy and professional obligations. Whilst this work is of critical importance, it can also reinforce unhelpful thinking, as (usually) professionals think that abuse is something that happens 'over there' and is committed only by aberrant or pathology ridden practitioners. What is clear from our work in this field, from published reports and from the stories bravely told in this book, is that so-called perpetrators have a range of intentions and circumstances that lead to serious violations of normal boundaries. Learning that focuses only on the 'over there' will have no impact on the individual who is at risk of stepping over the line. What is required is a language that connects the individual to the potential for harm. Using the notion that there is a spectrum of

Preface

professional boundaries and promoting the key skill of establishing and maintaining these boundaries has the potential to provide this connection.

Whether children's homes in Jersey, prisons in Iraq or hospitals in Cornwall, abuse of positions of trust is one of the biggest issues of our time; the stories told by survivors, as witnesses to their own abuse, provide the most powerful testimony possible, and the most compelling case for change.

Jonathan Coe
Chief Executive, WITNESS
April 2008

Foreword

The stories which follow are all very different but there are a number of threads which link them together. Each involves a person who was troubled and in need of help and who came to a helping professional or system for help and became ensnared in a complicated relationship.

As unique as each story may seem, there is none among them which is not remarkably similar to dozens of other cases seen at our center, the Walk-In Counseling Center in Minneapolis, Minnesota, USA, or described in the professional literature or the records of groups such as WITNESS. It would be preferable, of course, if these were rare and unique and exceptional, but sadly, they are not.

What is potentially confusing to both the client or patient, and those with whom they share their stories, is that in most if not all of these relationships the professional does in fact render help or care. In many instances this is quite "real" and often represents what feels at the time, and which may well be, comforting and helpful. Many times the professional actually stands out and seems to provide an exceptional quality of assistance. But let us start at the beginning.

Unfamiliar Territory
Amy Masters describes an abrupt awakening in an "alien environment" – in a psychiatric unit. She had lost everything and had confused thoughts,

and was clearly disoriented. Perhaps more dramatic than the other stories, but not completely unique in that in all of these cases the client or patient was in need of help and in most was going for a new type of help.

Clients do not know what psychotherapy or counselling are supposed to be like. They are usually working off of images from fiction, TV, or news media accounts. In some instances they may be comparing one practitioner with another, but in the bulk of stories in this volume they were newcomers to the helping process.

One does not go for counselling or psychotherapy, or even for most visits to a doctor, at the top of one's game. In fact, normally one is quite frightened and willing to trust a stranger with intimate details of one's life precisely because one is out of solutions and frightened. One is no longer able to manage one's life effectively. By definition one is willing to take a risk.

Michele Matheson, for example, sought help after a period of debilitating health problems – five abdominal surgeries accompanied by two different hormonal problems. She describes herself as a "rabbit caught in headlights" – what we term in the states "a deer in the headlights." Odd comments by her psychiatrist were presumed to be somehow therapeutic.

Louisa describes struggles with low self-confidence and a hope that hypnosis could provide her with a quick cure. When this didn't do the job, she found herself in an intensive psychodynamic therapy. The fact that much later she was to learn that the practitioner had faked his qualifications was irrelevant, because to her all of those letters after his name conveyed a sense of professional power. Even though she had actually read about the dynamics of the therapeutic relationship and "knew about" transference, the professional was in charge.

Judith Field sought to find the best therapist by checking on the beliefs of various possible care providers until she found one who seemed to stand out. She had found hugs reassuring and picked the one therapist who indicated that they were possible within the helping context. As the relationship began she felt that she had in fact picked the "right" therapist who could be helpful.

Jo Adams sought help while struggling with both depression and anxiety attacks. She had just six sessions with a practitioner which seemed to go well and be helpful. In her case had the professional relationship ended there things might have gone well, but he re-contacted her and pursued a relationship, extending his personal and professional contacts past what would have appeared to otherwise be a termination.

Help and Dependency

Melanie Cunningham sought and received support from her GP at a time of great personal distress and pressure – at the time of a divorce and custody struggle for her children. She had needs for emotional support and the GP provided this. This was not psychotherapy but given her needs and the situation it took its place. The doctor supported her in her at times lonely custody struggle but she became very dependent on him and became enmeshed in a personal and sexual relationship. Her level of vulnerability was great to start with, but her ongoing need for support kept her tied into the relationship and a pawn in the doctor's hands.

Amy Masters describes forming an attachment to her mental health worker built on her strong feeling that he was helping her. He spent time with her, took her on walks, and a trust and dependency developed. She had a great fear of losing him when she was discharged from the hospital.

Michele Matheson took a risk and trusted her psychiatrist, feeling that only full cooperation with his treatment regime could lead to a return to health. She became dependent on his judgments about her and found his praise to be like an addictive drug which made her feel very good. Louisa too felt that her therapist was a rescuer and she invested in his therapy, feeling that if she did so she would get better. Her whole life revolved around the treatment.

Judith Field felt that she was receiving special care, from hugs to a few extra minutes in a session, to small gifts, self-disclosure by the therapist, and other boundary crossings. She felt special. The therapist gave her a tape of the therapist talking to take with her, and eventually she was involved in both group and individual therapy. When the therapist diagnosed her family of origin as defective, a "re-birthing" was prescribed in order to undue these past experiences. The connection grew and continued for a number of years with Ms. Field experiencing her therapist as in some ways like a friend.

In the case of Jo Adams the sense that her contacts with a mental health worker had been helpful opened a door to her being grateful for his post-discharge attentions. However, this post-termination situation is just as confusing to a client or patient as the actual ongoing therapeutic relationship and she very easily lost her bearings. In this case, the power of the professional relationship continued even though formal meetings had ceased.

Special Powers – Transference

Having read about transference, Louisa knew what the term meant, but this in no way prepared her for dealing with it when it arose in her professional relationship. In fact it is the job of the professional to recognise transference and to assist the client in understanding it. Unfortunately, as in the cases in this book, all too often the professional is swept away by counter-transference and takes advantage of this power differential.

The existence and power of transference is well-recognised in American case law regarding sexual exploitation by therapists, and it is one of the reasons that nearly half of our states have made sexual exploitation of clients by psychotherapists a felony. (It is also a crime in a number of parts of Europe.) Transference is one of the phenomena which is thought to so distort the client's perception so as to render him or her unable to correctly judge what is happening.

While transference can involve negative feelings, in the cases in this volume it involves heightened positive feelings created by the client's perception being coloured by idealised images of the therapist as a trusted parent figure or spouse.

Unfortunately, often these feelings are so intense that they exceed those of a "normal" love relationship. Michele Matheson describes herself as feeling adored and worshipped and comments that she "never felt so lovely." The problem is that the feelings were very "real" and very strong – the type which cause the victim to feel that they never knew what "real love" was until now.

Jo Adams described her interaction with her Robert as powerful. Her depression lifted and she often felt elated. She tied her recovery to the relationship with him. Yet when she looked at him later, more objectively, she noted that he was singularly unattractive and so the idea that she could have been intimate with him was a surprise. This is a very common observation by victims after the fact.

The Professional is in Charge

Mental health and health care professionals have the power to interpret behaviour and create diagnostic labels. If they say you are ill, you are ill. If they say you are healthy, you are healthy. They can respond to challenges or criticisms or the fact that the client or patient is not getting better through some jargon-ridden explanation.

Although it was a non-sexual relationship with another woman, Judith Field clearly invested a great deal in her therapist with whom she felt very special. It was devastating when her therapist blamed her for anything which went wrong in the therapy – charging her with not trusting enough. Being a client in group, Judith also had to struggle with the fact that other clients supported the therapist's view of things.

Jo Adams describes how Robert, her mental health worker, joked about the rules on sexual involvement with former clients. She had no way of knowing what they were or how seriously they were taken. He was literally the person who could interpret the rules. It is noteworthy until about 20 years ago ethics codes tended to not even refer to the post-termination situation, and that during the last 20 years each profession has revised these rules. Each successive code change has become more conservative, lengthening the time which must pass or expanding the exclusions. The American Psychiatric Association, for example, has a standard which says it is never OK to have sex with a former patient, no matter how much time has elapsed since the last professional contact.

Michele Matheson's psychiatrist and Louisa's therapist began to eroticize those professional relationships and set the stage for boundary violations in each case using professional terms like "penis envy" or "sexual tension" very early in the therapeutic relationships.

The Nature of Consent
Rape or sexual assault is defined throughout the world as "non-consensual sex." This can be due to force or the threat of force, because the victim is too young to consent, because the victim is unconscious or medicated and unable to given consent, through fraud (e.g. sexual touch being falsely claimed to be a medical technique), etc. In US States and European countries where sexual contact between a therapist and client is a crime, it is considered sexual assault or rape. This is because *it is presumed to be non-consensual*. Quite specifically, in most of these statutes "consent is not a defence."

We start with the proposition that there is no earthly reason why such behaviour should be permitted and considerable evidence that it is typically harmful – *so there is no affirmative reason to allow it*. But the basis for saying that it cannot be consensual are several: (1) to have true consent, the client or patient needs to understand what is happening and its potential consequences; (2) the existence of transference distorts perception & judgment, and can render even an otherwise "high-powered" person as unable to correctly realise what is going on; (3) the power differential is substantial, both in terms of the power of the professional role and the dependency on professional help.

Thus, calling some of these relationships "affairs" is inaccurate and makes little sense. Sometimes news media, the public and even professionals slip into the use of this term because they are seeking to differentiate this behaviour from a violent, forcible rape. It is instructive in this regard to remember that one of the early psychiatric articles on this topic was Dr. Virginia Davidson's article "Psychiatry's problem with no name: Therapist-patient sex." (American Journal of Psychoanalysis, v. 37, 1977, pp. 43-50). Professionally I saw my first such case in 1968 and I remember well that I didn't know how to refer to it.

The concept of "an affair" involves a consensual relationship between two people who know what they are doing. Likewise, ending up living with the practitioner, or having a long relationship, or even marrying the professional does not change the reality as to how the relationship started. Nor do such actions alleviate the potential harm. This past year a client who married her therapist exploded and killed him after many years of marriage.

Pain, Pleasure, and the Road to Health
Returning to a relationship with an exploitive professional is normally a testament to dependency and often a belief that one cannot live without the professional. In dysfunctional professional relationships, clients are led to believe that their recovery if not their lives depend on the helper. In several of these stories it is clear that the client was fearful of being without the connection to the therapist. This belief is often encouraged by the professional, whereas in appropriate practice that professional should have been emphasising the client's own contributions to recovery.

As several of these stories indicate, and as noted above in the discussion of transference, some of these relationships are uniquely pleasurable and fulfilling. The vast majority involve many powerful feelings of love, sexual attraction, sexual pleasure – some to the level of a drug-like intoxication.

One of the most difficult issues in working with victims seeking to recover from such experiences is to help them understand how they could be so dependent and emotionally involved with the professional, or how they could have become sexually involved. Many cannot understand their own behaviour and often there is nothing in their life from which they can draw a comparison.

Often they find themselves having betrayed a spouse or family and having turned their back on a solid relationship which was "real" for this fantasy-laden and bizarrely intense involvement with someone who with hindsight is not the sort of person they would normally have the least attraction to.

In some relationships a type of masochistic bond is formed with the therapist playing the role of a sadist who punishes the client or patient. The client is dependent on the professional for a sense of self-worth and criticisms can be intensely painful. But because of low self-esteem, like the battered spouse who is a victim of domestic violence, the client returns for more punishment. Some of these relationships evolve into a mixture of pain and pleasure.

First Do No Harm
An early principle of Greek medicine was *first do no harm*. The Oath of Hippocrates, authored between the third and second centuries BC, states in part:

> *In to whatever homes I go, I go for the benefit of the sick, voluntarily abstaining from acts of mischief and corruption, and from the seduction of males or females, be they free men or slaves....*

Also relevant is a statement made in a TV interview by the chairman of the Maryland Board of Licensure for Physicians:

> *There is no medical condition which is improved by having the patient see the genitals of the doctor ....*

A great deal has been written about the harm caused by intense non-therapeutic emotional relationships or sexual relationships between helping professionals and their clients or patients. The cases which follow eloquently speak to these, but they include:

- The failure to render the care which was needed – the undermining of the basic therapeutic relationship (the client doesn't get the help she or he came for);
- Damage to trust in professionals and in others, which can also make it more difficult to get help;

- The need to receive treatment for the consequences of the abuse or exploitation – this can involve depression, various anxiety disorders including post-traumatic stress disorder (PTSD), guilt, shame, remorse, etc.
- Suicide attempts or completions
- A loss of relationships such as marriages which can never be reversed
- A loss of connection to ones children – missing key periods in their life and thus not fulfilling the parental role
- Loss of self-esteem, lack of trust in ones judgment, and general fearfulness
- The need to undergo lengthy and stressful complaint processes to achieve closure, justice, or to do one's civic duty

One of the challenges to those who seek to provide treatment for victims is the fact that the method used – psychotherapy – may be something which is now far more difficult due to fear. Some have compared it to taking a drink to cure a hangover. One also has the challenge of treating the original problems as well as the consequences of the abuse or exploitation – often in a situation where the supports (e.g. spouse) that the victim once had are no longer there.

Epilogue
In each of these stories the issue of obtaining justice or closure was a major challenge, which for the most part required some years of time and a stressful hearing before a body which was not presumed to be supportive. With a number of these cases the professional body did in fact side with the victim.

Actually, a number of these stories ended better than many, partly because these clients often had advocacy support. This underlines the importance of advocacy to even ensure that such hearings occur and that there is a reasonable chance that the complainant will be heard.

In Amy Masters' case there is a contrast with how the offender's employer, a hospital, dealt with the case as compared with the NMC which believed her and which did not use the flawed rationale the hospital did to decide that a lesser penalty would be sufficient.

Gary R. Schoener, M.Eq., Licensed Psychologist
Executive Director, Walk-In Counseling Center, Minneapolis, Minnesota
USA, December 2007

1

Amy Masters

The Horror of Hospital

The realisation suddenly dawned on me when I woke up. I was in a psychiatric ward. The events of the previous night were just a blur. The admission process had been intimidating, lengthy and intrusive and I was tired and scared. I was in a dormitory with three strangers, an alien environment in which I didn't belong.

Confused and tangled thoughts were rushing through my mind. What was I doing here? How on earth had I ended up in this place? I'd known about it all my life - it was the place for 'mad people' and was to be feared and avoided, I didn't belong here. I felt as if I had lost everything – my career, my fiancé, my future, even the motivation to live.

I was in this place where people were 'locked up' – I didn't know what was going to happen to me, how long I was going to be here or even whether anyone would talk to me. I was so alone.

I had moved back to my hometown after seven years in Southampton, four of which included a degree course. I'd been suffering from depression after the break up of my relationship and the pressure of a demanding course. It had all become too much. Three years of sporadic input from the mental health teams had hardly helped me and I was now living in a damp bed-sit away from friends and family. This contributed to the decline in my mental state and took me to the brink of death through suicide attempts and increasingly dangerous self-harm. I was also losing control of a well-established eating disorder.

I moved back to my hometown, albeit in a rather cold and depressing flat, but at least I was near those who I had known for a long time and with whom I felt safe.

A year after I moved back, it was clear that I wasn't able to cope on my own, so I stayed with some good friends for a while. I wasn't functioning very well and would hide in my room, unable to interact much or participate in meals with the family. The days seemed end less and lonely and many times I would just walk aimlessly for hours, not knowing where I was going. My self-harm had reached a dangerous level, both in terms of the frequency and severity. I was causing my friends much concern, so much so that they took advice and contacted the on-call duty psychiatrist. That's how I found myself in hospital. I endured a two hour wait for the psychiatrist to arrive at my friends' home and when he arrived he began to 'interrogate' me, asking me questions on many issues that were painful to recall. I then had to go through a similar process with the hospital doctor. It all made me feel exposed and vulnerable.

I heard a voice, "Good morning Amy, time to get up!" The curtains around me were flung back and Mo, a Health Care Assistant, introduced herself to me. I was relieved that someone was talking to me at last. She told me where things were and said that breakfast would be in half an hour. It was all so frightening. I managed to get dressed but I couldn't bear the thought of eating, and certainly not in a room full of people, and anyway, I hadn't been told where the dining room was.

The first couple of days in the hospital were like being in some awful nightmare; I was scared of everyone and longed to wake up and see friends and familiar surroundings. I kept asking myself; what was the purpose of me being here? Why did no member of staff talk to me, other than to inform me of meal times and medication? Was being in this terrifying place supposed to make me feel better? I'd been told that I was a voluntary patient, but if I tried to run away, would I be sectioned 'for my own safety?' I felt this powerful tension rising up in me and I was scared that the release of it would be explosive and destructive.

I was then introduced to John, who was to be my key worker. I didn't know what that meant but hoped that at last I would be able to talk to someone who could help me to feel less desperate in this bewildering place.

John was quite friendly and had a calming voice. I was scared at first as I had grown up without a father and was wary of men. I had not had good experiences in my relationships. The ending of my engagement destroyed any trust I had and I had since become involved with another man in Southampton where we had become emotionally co-dependant. It was not a healthy relationship; we were both mentally very unwell and had made a suicide pact. Part of the reason for my moving was to break the stranglehold we had over each other.

At first, John made me feel safe. He made specific time every day to talk to me – and he kept to his word. The days still seemed endless, but I would watch the clock, counting the minutes until my key-working session with John. Although I still hated the hospital environment, I slowly became familiar with my surroundings and managed as best as I could. I became quite obsessive in my routine each day, paying meticulous attention to making my bed (with 'hospital corners!'), showering at the same time every day, taking time over my hair and so on. Part of it was to pass the time, but it was really about trying to maintain come control in this very restrictive environment.

When John talked to me, I felt that he was genuinely interested in how I was. I was brave enough to talk about Matthew in Southampton and how the relationship was still causing me great anguish. John asked me a lot of questions, particularly about my relationships and specifically the physical and sexual aspect of them. This made me feel very uncomfortable. I was not used to talking to a man about such personal things, but John persisted. I had not slept with either my fiancé or Matthew because for me, sex was for marriage. John mocked me for this and held no regard for my views or my Christian faith. He called me 'the ice queen,' and in my naivety I didn't know what he meant by this.

However in spite of this, I still wanted to talk to John. He did spend quite a bit of time with me. On the ward I was missing being able to exercise and not eating because of concerns over my weight. John took me on walks, just the two of us, within and beyond the hospital grounds. One walk I remember took us some way from the hospital. I remember reading one of the road signs and thinking that we had walked a very long way. I was a bit scared and felt vulnerable. I was also quite weak from lack of food and wondered if I'd make it back to the ward. John seemed quite concerned about my physical state – he observed that I was losing weight and talked to me about 'The Programme' for eating disorders. He said that if I went below a certain weight I would be put on the programme where I would have to eat five times a day, be observed while eating and be weighed in just my underwear. This terrified me and in my naivety I believed him. I know now that I would have had to have a considerably lower BMI (Body Mass Index) than I had to be subjected to that. I was horrified at the thought of being weighed – and in my underwear! I had nightmares of being forcefully dragged to the scales, kicking and screaming against the total humiliation.

John talked to me a lot about my concerns with how I looked. He told me that *he* liked me even though in most people's opinions I was too thin. He argued that if he liked me as I was, then surely others could. He was convinced that I denied myself food to make myself lose weight, deliberately becoming too thin in order to be unattractive to men; hence 'protecting' myself from them, and from sex - which he believed I feared. He also said to me on one occasion that he had a 'fascination with female anorexic cutters.' I found the use of the word 'fascination' quite disturbing.

I listened to what John said but was not always sure that I agreed with him. He made comments and posed questions that really made me question myself. I was in a very unsettled state of mind and he was the professional – maybe everything he said was right? I hated myself and was on a path of self-destruction. The few relationships with men that I'd had were all difficult in different ways and yes, after finding about my fiancé's affair, I strongly believed that I would never trust a man again. However, in the 'safe' environment of the hospital where I had come to hope that I would be helped to feel better, there was John; a man with whom I found myself sharing painful and personal details of my life and who really seemed to listen to me. Even though he asked me some odd (and maybe inappropriate) questions, I came to see him as a 'safe' man who was looking after me. I developed a trust and dependence and felt a need for him to be there; not only in key-worker sessions, but during the day when I was upset and experiencing the urge to self-harm, he was there for me. The most difficult days were when he had a day off and the hours dragged and I had no one to talk to.

I did have quite a few visitors and they too made the hospital stay more bearable. They provided a link to the outside world. They accepted me as I was and reassured me that I wasn't going completely mad. Visitors were the highlight of my day, but John took priority. If he had arranged to see me at a certain time and a visitor arrived, I became anxious, worrying that I'd lost my opportunity to speak to him that day. I had developed an attachment to him because I believed he was helping me.

After the initial shock at finding myself in hospital, I felt somewhat relieved because all responsibility was taken from me. I didn't have to worry about the necessary, mundane tasks of life like laundry, washing up and cleaning and there were no real demands or expectations on me. I was in hospital because I was not well. The outside world had become unsafe for me; I had stopped being able to function properly, my mind had become consumed with thoughts of destroying myself. My weeks had been punctuated by trips to A&E, which served only to lower my opinion of myself and convince me further that my life was not worth living- I had reached a place of despair and uncertainty about whether I wanted to carry on. Being in the hospital gave me space to rest, and try to get the self-harm under control. I knew I couldn't do it on my own, I needed help, and John was there.

We talked at great length about my cutting. It had become a way of dealing with unmanageable emotions and a way of punishing myself, I felt a complete and utter failure. It was something I did impulsively, mindlessly and with no regard for the damage I was causing myself. John seemed very keen to talk about it, but that was hard as it had always been something very secret that I did in private and it carried with it unbearable shame. I did not want to talk about it or reveal my scars, but John was the professional and so I talked to him, trusting that he would not tell me off or lock me away, but would help me get through this nightmare I was living.

I had not thought that much about why I cut myself and what it did for me. I didn't have a level of cognitive functioning that would have enabled me to do that. All I could say to John was that I just felt this enormous tension or wave of emotion (which I couldn't name or describe) which was absolutely overwhelming and lead to me to violent impulsive actions directed solely at myself.

John had his own ideas about why I cut – ideas that horrified me and had never entered my mind. He talked about my lack of sexual experience and told me that my cutting was a form of masturbation. I cannot adequately put into words my reaction to this. Although I had not been able to talk about the cutting or try to question it myself at that point, there was *never* any thought in my mind that my cutting was for sexual

31

gratification. This did make me feel extremely uncomfortable. I could not relate to what John was saying and because of later events, I have since wondered if these thoughts and images were turning him on.

I remember expressing my horror at this interpretation of my cutting, but John pursued his thoughts saying that I was in denial and was a sexually repressed female who cut herself because she was scared of sex with men.

I knew that this was not the reason I cut myself, but felt that John thought he was right. It worried me that he thought of me in this way – I felt unclean and exposed and I tried to think about what he was 'seeing' in his mind when he thought of me cutting myself. It was impossible for me to imagine really as I could not relate to it at all.

Even after this I still trusted John and felt that I needed him to be there for me. Increasingly I found some of his thoughts very challenging, causing me to doubt my own sanity, but I still believed he would help me – after all, he was the professional, the nurse who was looking after me.

At one ward-round the psychiatrist was there along with John and a whole room of people I'd never met and they began to talk about my discharge. I don't remember much about that meeting except that I felt terrified at thought of going home, being on my own and not being able to talk to John. My care plan was discussed and it was agreed that I would be referred to a clinical psychologist but that the waiting time would be at least ten months.

I could not contemplate going home with no hope of support for ten months. Although I had felt safe in hospital, I did not feel safe at the prospect of going back to my flat. But I felt guilty for all the worry that I'd given my friends, and so felt that I should return. I told John that I was scared and didn't know how I would manage and could not cope with the thought of losing his support.

John 'reassured' me and said he would 'see me privately.'

Beyond the Boundaries
I was discharged into my world of fear and self-destructive behaviour. Being in hospital had not helped me to find other ways of coping, nor had it lifted me out of the pit of despair. I still felt hopeless. I was home, feeling desperate at the thought of waiting ten months for therapy but counting on John being there for me to help me through. I didn't see him outside of the hospital until a month after discharge, but during that time

Amy Masters

I wrote to him at the hospital, talking about my feelings and reflecting on what we talked about. I could not detach myself from him. He knew things about me that no one else knew and I felt that this gave him some power over me. I felt that I needed him and could not imagine surviving the wait for therapy. I wrote a few letters talking about what had happened and trying to sort out in my head how I saw him – 'a safe bloke?', 'a father figure?'

He eventually replied to my letters, a very short letter that included the following;

Dear Amy,

Hi, I have received and read your letters. I must admit feeling that something happened when we met. I still am confused over the whole matter. I do find myself thinking about you rather a lot . . . . . . I look forward to receiving your next letter.

This was very closely followed by an even shorter letter from his *wife*, telling me to stop writing to John otherwise he would 'loose' his job. (The teacher in me always remembers spelling mistakes!) This letter made me feel very scared and vulnerable. Obviously she had read my letters – how could he betray my trust? How did she obtain my home address? Would she come round and threaten me? It really unnerved me.

John contacted me by phone and arranged to meet me at 4.30pm in the local park. We talked about what it had been like for me since discharge and how my self-harm had increased again. I believed that I was safe with John and that he really wanted to help me. I think there was part of me that thought that meeting like this was not the usual thing, but he had offered to 'see me privately' and it was nothing to do with the hospital. (Or so I told myself).

We met in the park on twelve occasions over five months and John would phone me sometimes. We talked about many things including my memories from my childhood, relationships with my family and with men, my eating disorder, how I saw my future etc. I was surprised at how much work and time John put into our meetings. I had told him things that I had previously kept secret. I had been assaulted when I was thirteen and this had made a huge impact on me; adding to my already established fear of men and leading to an intense fear of rape – in my mind, any man walking by on the street was a potential attacker so I lived in constant fear. I wasn't afraid of John because he listened to me and gave me time. He set me 'homework tasks' and I worked hard on them – to please him I guess, and to show that I was grateful for all the time he was giving to me. One task he set me was as follows:

Consider - document if required, a wanted (preferred) future.
Try brainstorming – Goal 30 ideas
1. Nun

This task in itself was reasonable but his sarcastic suggestion of 'becoming a Nun' had its roots in his opinion of my views on sex before marriage and his description of me as 'the ice queen'. He constantly referred to my Christian faith in a negative or mocking way which upset me very much. An extract from another of his letters says,

I have asked you if you think you are a masochist. What does your faith say about what some would see as unusual sexual practices?

So here he was again, pursuing his idea that my cutting was for sexual gratification. It continued to upset me but, as time was to show, John did not let go of his thoughts and fantasies.

As the summer turned into autumn it got cold sitting in the park. I remember shivering on a bench in the dark in early October. John put his arm around me and I remember feeling safe and warm, but as it got colder, we met in the café in the park and talked and drank tea. On one occasion someone came up to John in the café and said hello. He looked very uncomfortable – maybe she was a family friend or a colleague from work, I don't know. It wasn't long after that, in mid November, that John started to see me at my flat. It was always 4.30pm or 5.30pm depending on when he left work. There it was easier to do some 'work.' John produced some sheets on the computer with different things written on them and we discussed them and put 'post-it' notes all over them. I was really impressed that he took so much time thinking about the work that he was doing with me. I found it a challenge and looked forward to each time we met. I thought he genuinely cared about me . . . Little did I know at that time, he was doing a Counselling Course and was using me as a client *without* my knowledge or consent. No wonder he was so diligent in his work.

One night I was very upset and John put his arm round me. My emotions were so stirred up with painful memories; I knew that I would feel the need to cut myself later on if the level of intensity didn't subside. I didn't want John to go because I was so scared of my emotions that had been unearthed during the evening and I wanted John to stay a bit longer until I felt better. He held me in his arms, very close and he kissed me. It was a shock to me, not only that it happened, but that I had reciprocated. I felt a whole mixture of things, from shame and disgust to actually liking it. (I have to say at this point that admitting that I liked it is very difficult because it brings me back into all the thoughts of guilt and blaming myself and wishing I'd never met him outside the hospital.) He tasted of pipe tobacco, which was horrible, but at the same time I felt strangely safe and secure in the arms of a man in who I'd put my trust and who knew some of my well-kept secrets.

I had shared with John my intense fear of rape and recounted a situation with a boy from school. The boy had met me in the field at the back of my garden at home and had pinned me to the floor and was on top of me, taunting me. He said, 'This is what you and Andrew have been up to isn't it?" I was terrified – I had never had this experience with Andrew. He was a boy I 'went out with' when I was 11 years old. Four of us from school would hang out together and go to each other's houses and all we got up to was kissing each other on the lips, which we thought was rather naughty and daring. The incident with the other boy stayed with me and I would revisit it in nightmares where I would wake up struggling for breath. I'd had so little experience with men during my childhood with no father around – my mother had clearly communicated to me that they were all bastards and not to be trusted. This experience and then the assault at the age of thirteen convinced me that men were unsafe, cruel and frightening.

I didn't feel that about John. I guess that in spite of my thoughts about men, there was still that longing for a 'safe' man; one that could feel the deep aching gap that had been left by my father just before I was born. I wanted to be held and cuddled and be told that everything would be OK, by someone strong and able to contain the pain and hurts that were tearing me apart.

But the boundaries and the relationship with John had changed. The long intimate kiss made it all confusing. I was still that little child, hurting and wanting to be picked up by a strong father figure, but at the same time, an adult, who was talking about personal things with another adult. John chose to focus on issues to do with men. When I talked about experiences I'd had, he asked me more questions and wanted more details.

I wrote a diary during this time and following the kiss I wrote this:

Broken Boundaries

The kiss didn't cause me to want to run away – I wanted to stay; in fact, it felt good. I went to the gym feeling very mixed up. I cried all the way there. While I was running, I had the desire to cut badly, there and then. I didn't know why, because much of what I had in my mind regarding John was good. I was embarrassed and angry with myself for not doing the homework as I owe it to John to make an effort. He is investing time in helping me . . .

Suffice it to say, the diary for that day continued with a somewhat confused inner dialogue, ending with a graphic description of a severe self-harming episode, resulting in an overnight stay at the general hospital.

I was in turmoil; my weakened physical state was not helping my mental state and I was questioning whether I was getting any better. I believed what John was saying to me in terms of my progress and now of course, I had the complication of what the kiss meant. I was wracked with guilt every time I thought about it and admitted to myself that I liked it. I should not have liked it. I was wrong, bad and should have resisted. Aside from the fact that he was a professional and supposed to be helping me, he was married for goodness sake, and that would always be forbidden territory. But why was I even thinking like this? The kiss should never have happened full stop – because of the nature of the relationship. Had it now ruined everything? I couldn't bear how I was feeling – I had cut myself badly but it hadn't made me feel better. Who else could I turn to, what else could I do? I had good friends at Church; a couple who I really trusted, but I couldn't even bring myself to tell them. I was so wrong, so bad, but right from the start, my meetings with John had been very secret – 'clandestine' was the word he used.

After the horror of the overnight stay in hospital, a badly damaged wrist and a five-hour wait to be interrogated by a duty psychiatrist, I came home and was wondering if I would see John again. I was never allowed to contact him – I just had to wait. The next day I wrote in my diary;

I am relieved to have heard from John today; partly because I haven't been waiting around a long time for a phone call, wondering if he's 'abandoned' me – and partly because I want to discuss Friday with him.

There is a gap in my memory about what we did say about 'the kiss' – maybe we didn't say anything? I was feeling vulnerable and wanted John to be there for me. It usually took me a few days to recover from a significant blood loss and I guess my physical weakness and bandaged arm communicated that I needed, wanted, to be looked after.

We certainly continued with the work, but my diaries were recording more and more confusion about everything – my relationship with John, whether I was working hard enough with him, how my Christian faith linked with everything else in my life, what my eating disorder was about . . . and so on, over and over again.

However, the big change was the development from the kiss and hug in the doorway through to much more physical and then sexual contact. One evening I was sat in the chair and John was on the floor with all the paperwork (for his course, unbeknown to me) and when he'd finished he put his head in my lap and I touched his hair. I knew at that point that this was not OK, but it was as if John had power over me and I still felt that he was safe and would do nothing to harm me. As the weeks went on, he would arrive at the same time after work but stay increasingly late, sometimes beyond ten o'clock. One evening the phone rang and it was his wife asking to speak to him, as he should have been home some time ago. I had no idea at that time that she knew he was coming to see me as a 'client' and obviously knew that a 5.30pm session should not last five hours. I was very scared and alarmed by her angry tone and felt as if she was an angry wife discovering her husband's sordid affair. I lived in fear that she would come to my flat and beat me up or something.

In spite of this, John still came round and still stayed late. What began as kissing and hugging developed into John touching me. I didn't know what to do, part of me wanted to make him feel good, as he'd helped me so much, but I was shy and embarrassed. We would do 'the work' and John would say, 'now we can get on with the sex bit'. I found it really hard to cope with. I had always been very self-conscious, was sexually inexperienced and hated the thought of anyone getting close to me as I felt fat, ugly and was badly scarred. John would gently caress my body and begin to undo my clothes above the waist. My body would freeze in fear but he would say, 'I won't hurt you . . .' One evening he was sat astride me and I had a vivid flashback to the episode I had described to him about the boy in the playing field. John knew a lot about my experiences with men and I wondered if he was trying to act them out. I felt trapped and suffocated, just as I did when I was twelve. However I did let him do things to me but with intense fear that he would eventually force me to have sex with him. I had thoughts in my mind that he knew that I had a fear of rape and he knew I'd never had sex, so perhaps he was planning to teach me something. One night when I was lying on the floor, naked above the waist and John was on top of me; he looked at me and said, "I can imagine myself cutting you all over." To this day, this is the one thing that continues to freak me out. I've had countless nightmares when I've woken up, dripping in sweat but thinking that I was covered in blood. It's a vivid experience every time. I believe that John wanted to act out his own bizarre and disgusting fantasies. He made it clear that cutting me all over would be for mutual sexual gratification. I still cannot imagine that it would have done anything for me, other than evoke terror, and of course, cause me physical damage . . . and more scars. I am totally convinced that had he acted this out I would not have been able to live with it and would have taken my life. Sometimes, even now, I think that that is the only way I can be free from the memories and images, forever.

When the intensity of the sexual activity increased, John asked me if I was on the Pill. It was then that I was really scared and knew that he wanted to have sex with me. Perhaps it would have given him a buzz, having sex with a virgin.

I'm sure that the fact that I wasn't on the pill deterred him going that far – after all, if I became pregnant, people would know about his own particular style of 'counselling.' It wasn't long after that, that John started to talk about 'ending' with seeing me. I was shocked and upset, it was January and he said that we would finish at Easter. I was very scared about what might happen. Although I felt that I needed John, there had been an increasing concern that he wasn't being 'therapeutic' – even he said that once in a letter. It's difficult to describe, but even though I wasn't happy about some of the things that he'd said and done, there was a powerful dependence in which I felt trapped. All the sexual stuff that was happening caused me much shame and guilt, I felt disgusted with myself. The cutting increased and my mental state deteriorated. We continued to do some work (obviously he had to produce something for his case study on me) but there was more and more time spent having sexual contact. He left a month between the penultimate and final session (in true counselling fashion) and on that last day we spent many hours together and I was in a desperate state, not wanting him to leave, not knowing how I'd cope without him. He told me that I had the support of an Occupational Therapist so would be OK while I waited for the psychological support.

I was totally in pieces feeling desperate, abandoned and very frightened. I didn't know how to process all that had happened. Any of the 'work' we had done seemed irrelevant. I still didn't know until years later that he didn't care about me, but was using me as a counselling client and feeding his own sexual fantasies at my expense.

In November of that same year, I was re-admitted to the hospital. It was around the time of my birthday, which held some painful memories for me. As the ward where patients go corresponds to where they live, I was back on John's ward. I cannot begin to describe how awful that was. Part of me was terrified of John and part of me wanted him to look after me again, but he totally ignored me. The hospital stay simply exacerbated my inner anguish and though it was deemed to be a place of safety for me, I felt extremely exposed and vulnerable.

My next admission was a few months later when I was admitted to a different ward, much to my relief, but then I was told that I would be moving to my Consultant's ward, where John was still. I became very distressed and pleaded not to be moved to that ward, but there was no negotiation. I kept on and on protesting but it was going to happen regardless. A male nurse asked me why I didn't want to move and I said that there was a nurse there that I didn't like. I didn't want to say any more about it but he persisted, 'who was it, why didn't I like him?' Under much pressure I blurted out that he was my key nurse and I got attached to him last time I was in hospital and I didn't want to get upset again. This nurse wore me down with his questioning and asked me who it was. He promised not to tell any one so I said it was John. He went away immediately and came back with one of the hospital managers who wanted to know what the problem was with John. I remember being quite alarmed at this – this was one of the 'big-wigs' here, I had to be careful what I said. I wouldn't have dreamed of saying anything about what had happened for fear that I would be in serious trouble. I was also very angry because the nurse had said he wouldn't tell anyone – my trust had been broken yet again by a man. I played down my 'dislike' of John and it ended up that I was moved to that ward but John would not be my key nurse.

So as well as the events that had led up to this admission – severe emotional chaos and another dangerous cutting episode, I had to manage all the stuff that went with being near *him* and a reliving of the memories of what had happened between us. It was hell.

I had mixed up, irrational thoughts about John; part of me was finding it hard to detach and part of me could not bear the thought of being near him ever again. When I had been seeing him, I'd talked about suicide and felt that it was something that was inevitable as I could see no future and no hope of recovery. John wanted to know the details of my plan – it was frightening for me to verbalise the thoughts I had in my mind, but at the time I trusted him, I told him that the worst thing about committing suicide was the thought of dying alone. I even asked him if he would be with me when I did it. He said that he could only do that if I had gone beyond the point of being saved or resuscitated. The picture was clear in my mind, where I would be, where John would be and so on.

When he stopped seeing me I was left with an intolerable amount of emotion that I couldn't process or understand. I felt desperately alone as this was 'our secret' and I was ashamed to tell even my most trusted friends. I was gradually talking myself into taking my life as I saw no other way to cope with it. I started going to the hospital at the end of the evening shift waiting for John to leave work. I'd cycle down there in the dark and wait – my intention was to throw myself in front of his motorbike so he could 'finish me off.' He had already damaged me beyond repair, I didn't care anymore. I didn't want it to be as I'd previously planned, with John by my side, holding my hand while I died – no, I wanted him to be the one that had a hand in my death and would have that on his conscience forever. I would drug myself up with my medication before so that I wouldn't gain consciousness when I was knocked over. I don't know how many times I skulked around the hospital after dark – on a few occasions John saw me and stopped and talked to me. Part of me wanted him to see me . . . I didn't know what I wanted really. I started to wait some way up the road so that he would be riding at some speed when he hit me, but I never had the courage to follow through what I'd planned.

The 'Secret Years'

This is the period of time up until when I had the courage to speak about what had happened. I kept all the details to myself; it was like some 'sordid secret' that I held on to very tightly for fear of judgement and condemnation. I continued to think about what had happened and had recurrent nightmares about him cutting me all over. I felt that I only had myself to blame as I had 'encouraged him' and wanted to continue seeing him. I wished that he'd never offered to see me privately but at the same time, I knew that I had become dependent on him and couldn't imagine not having him there to talk to.

Another very difficult aspect with all of this was that I was beginning to get involved in 'Service User' work in the Hospital. I attended various meetings as a service user rep, I was involved in service user interviews with patients on the wards and had begin to participate in Trust training, giving the Service User perspective.

This meant that there were numerous opportunities to bump into John as I moved around the hospital. I never really felt safe and when those chance 'meetings' did happen I usually got away as soon as I could and broke down and sometimes cut myself. I was doing some work on the wards once and was taken to the staff dining room for lunch with a student nurse. I really did not want to go. It felt very uncomfortable seeing staff who had nursed me when I was an inpatient. Then I saw John – he made a comment on the fact that I was only eating a banana. I went red with shame and struggled to get through that half hour, shaking and fighting back the tears.

I found it so hard continuing the work at the hospital, but it was important to me. I had had several admissions and was at last seeing the long awaited psychologist. I wanted to be 'doing something' even though I had to admit that I wasn't ready for paid employment. I received an invitation to join a user group whose aim was to enable people to have their say about how services were run and to be involved in planning and implementing new ones. Over the coming years I was to gain in confidence and become quite well known within the Trust. I was determined that all that had happened with John was not going to stop me doing this work that I was beginning to enjoy, but it was at great cost to me emotionally.

On one occasion I was attending a Clinical Governance meeting where the Policy on 'Sexual Harassment' was being discussed. One person was talking about patients who 'behave inappropriately' towards staff. It was clear that the thought of any member of staff having sexual feelings for patients was unthinkable. I could not stay in the room so left in tears.

I continued to do the work, gaining back some of the confidence I had lost through my mental health problems and was thrilled to find that I could write papers on mental health issues and re-awaken my dormant teaching skills. I loved the work, but any Trust activity always carried with it the fear that one day I might encounter John at a training session or a meeting. I could not imagine how I would handle it.

I lived with the guilt and shame that tormented me for eight years. I had only vaguely mentioned to two trusted church friends that something had happened to me, but I didn't share any details or give a name. I was terrified of the consequences and was totally convinced that no one would believe me – after all, he was the professional and I was just a mental health patient who could have simply dreamed it all up. I would never have thought of my experience as abuse. I knew the experience had left me screwed up inside, experiencing nightmares and flashbacks, living in constant fear of seeing John and dealing with my emotions as a result, but I largely blamed myself. I was full of 'if only's – if only I hadn't gone for walks with him, if only I hadn't let myself get attached, if only I'd never let him into my flat. It was all my fault; there was no point telling anyone as they would tell me just that, "Well, you've only got yourself to blame . . ."

Breaking the Silence

I was facilitating a 'Focus group' at the Psychological therapies service, asking people to talk about their experiences of therapy and to comment on the service as a whole. One woman there dominated the group and was extremely angry. She recounted her experience with a male psychologist who used to talk to her about her sexual relationships and comment on her physical appearance with sexual innuendo. She used the word 'abuser' many times and felt that he 'was getting off on it,' talking to her in great detail about sexual things. She went on throughout the group about how she'd reported him and no one believed her, and how she was going to sue the Trust and that he wasn't going to get away with it.

I listened carefully as I was taken back in my mind to how John used to speak to me and focus on sexual things. I was amazed at this woman's outspoken nature and how she was totally convinced that she had been abused. I found myself thinking, 'you're right' he was out of order, and this led me to think of John – was what I went through, 'abuse??'

She said that she had been in contact with an organisation called POPAN (Prevention of Professional Abuse Network) for help and advice. She spoke very positively about them, as they listened and understood. I felt my heart beating faster and wondered if I would have the courage at the end of the group to ask her for POPAN's address. It did indeed take a lot of courage because I didn't just want to say could I have the details because they sounded interesting. I wanted to hear myself say, for the first time, that I might have been *abused* – and say it to someone I knew could identify with me and who would not judge me.

I kept the details for a long time but then contacted the help line, only to hear the voice of a *man* at the other end. It was incredibly hard to talk, but his gentle, calm voice helped me to feel able to say a little, and by the end of the conversation I was clear about the notion of professional boundaries – and knew that John had totally overstepped them.

However, I was nowhere near a point where I would have considered reporting him or making a formal complaint. I just knew that I wanted to talk about it more and convince myself it wasn't totally my fault. I had developed a good relationship with my psychologist and was undergoing Cognitive Analytic Therapy (CAT) with her. I tentatively began to talk to her about what had happened but was very careful not to mention his name. She made it very clear that if I said his name, she would have no choice but to report him. As I talked I became more convinced that yes, he was in the wrong and, even if I had begged him to see me, he should have said no, as he was the professional and had the responsibility not to overstep the professional boundaries. Her visible reaction to some of what I described served to convince me more that what I had experienced was abuse.

As I talked with my psychologist, I was able, for the first time, to talk about some of the painful memories and to cry in a safe place with a therapist whom I trusted. She assured me that if I chose to do anything about it, i.e. making a formal complaint, or not, she would support me.

It took a lot more talking and thinking about whether I would make a formal complaint. I made contact with the Mental Health Advocacy Service, and spoke to them in vague terms about my case. I wanted to test to see if they could help me, and after our conversation, I was totally reassured that they could. I then spoke to the Associate Nurse Director (Mr A.N.D.) of in-patient services to talk about making a formal complaint about a member of the nursing staff. He suggested that it might be helpful to talk to someone who no longer worked with the Trust but who would perhaps help me come to a decision of whether to take it forward or not. I knew the person he was suggesting, and felt that I would be OK speaking to her. Throughout all these discussions, John's name was never mentioned, but it was getting increasingly hard to stop myself saying it accidentally.

It took six months after the focus group to make the huge decision to make a formal complaint. I remember going to a cold dreary office to meet Mr A.N.D. for inpatient services, and read out a précised version of what had happened. I sat there at the beginning with clammy hands and a dry throat. I took a deep breath and started, "I want to talk about what happened with John ＿＿＿＿ " The Manager just said in a slow deliberate way, "Right . . . . ." I wanted to know if he was shocked or surprised when I gave the name. I was taken, in my mind, to that time on the ward where he was stood at the foot of my bed asking me what the problem was with John when I was refusing to move wards. Why did he come so quickly and why was I asked so many questions at that time?

Somehow I managed to get through what I'd written and then just broke down. This was the first time I had spoken about some of the stuff and of course, the first time I had mentioned John's name, knowing full well that this would have serious consequences.

Although I'd attended that initial meeting alone, from then on I always had the support of the Advocate at every subsequent meeting. Looking back, there was no way that I could have gone through the process unsupported, it would just have been too much.

I had spoken his name, and so the silence was broken.

The Investigation

The Trust's policy states that any member of staff under investigation will be suspended on full pay and without prejudice for the duration of the investigation. The day after I spoke to the Manager, John was suspended. The policy also states that during the period of suspension, a person is not allowed on Trust premises.

A week later I was involved in interviewing staff as a service user member of the panel. This was a part of my post at the Trust. I arrived at the building to be met by the sight of John's distinctive motorbike. I went to pieces and couldn't go in. I was crying and shaking whilst I phoned the appointing officer, Alistair, to say that I couldn't come into the building. He came to get me and I said with great reluctance that I had made a complaint about John and that I knew he was in the building and I was too scared to go in.

He said, "Oh don't worry, he's on the top floor and we'll be on the second."

By this time I was sobbing uncontrollably. I was taken upstairs and left in a big room still crying while Alistair went off to do some photocopying. I could not hold back my tears, I was so scared that I went and hid in the toilets. Hopefully there was no chance of seeing John there. When I plucked up the courage to return to the room, another interviewer had appeared and said, "Oh, are you alright?" I said no, but he chose not to respond.

Amy Masters

I will never know how I got through those interviews, I was as calm and professional as I ever was, but it was at great cost emotionally and I cut myself as soon as I got home – I simply didn't know what else to do.

The advocate was appalled to hear of my experience, especially as the terms of John's suspension had been breached. When challenged by the Advocate, Alistair simply said, "Oh, he was just using my office to make some phone calls, I'm his Union Rep." ('Oh' indeed, so that's OK is it? Not only was John not supposed to be on Trust premises, he had been working with Alistair up to the moment I had arrived. Alistair knew jolly well that I was going to be in the building that day. He was probably with John when I was outside crying on the phone to him.) My Advocate was given no explanation as to why this had been allowed.

The next blow was to learn that John was back to work after being suspended for just two weeks. The investigation was to go on for much, much longer. This was a complete breaching by the Trust of its own policy. When we challenged this we were given the reply, 'There are some situations where staff under investigation can go back to work, and this is one of them. He was not deemed to be a risk to patients so could continue to work in the same hospital, on the same ward'.

I was devastated – so there it was; I had to attend meetings regarding the investigation in the same building as my abuser who was still working with vulnerable people – it made me sick. Quite soon, however, most of the meetings with the investigating officer – Mr A.N.D. himself, did take place away from the hospital site, which was better.

Two weeks after the initial conversation with Mr A.N.D. I met with him again and he informed me that the matter could be 'done and dusted' fairly quickly and that I may not need to be involved. (WHAT? Done and dusted? Swept under the carpet I supposed.) I was told that John had not denied that *something* had happened, but if I was not involved much in the investigation, it would all be done behind closed doors and he would probably get a slap on the wrist and be told not to do it again.

However I was involved with further meetings - to clarify my statement and to try and find out what the next steps would be. The investigating officer took no notes at any of these meetings, so I decided to take a voice recorder so that I would be able to refer to it later on.

The meetings were very stressful and frustrating. My advocate was present every time and was a great support, asking questions and doing her best to make sure I was fully informed of the next steps. (I asked the Investigating Officer several questions to which he gave only vague answers, or none at all.) It was frustrating to say the least. I was struggling to keep up with all the things that I'd been involved with. It was hard to switch off between meetings and maintain some sense of normality. I had extra support from the psychologist, beyond the ending of the CAT therapy, which was a tremendous help, but it didn't take away the strain of going through the lengthy process. Everything seemed fraught with uncertainty and felt to be going on forever.

Then there seemed to be a lull in proceedings. After more letters, phone calls and e-mails I was told that the disciplinary procedure was on hold 'due to reasons beyond our control.' (I found out that John had gone off sick for a number of weeks.)

Six months had passed and still there was no date for the hearing, still I did not know who was taking the lead for organising panel members. There was a real likelihood that I would know most of the panel members from my service user work, which would make it very difficult for me. I knew it was going to be an internal employment hearing - them against me.

The date was set – and rescheduled – five times. I was told that I would be sent information outlining the expectations and procedures, including the agenda, the names of the panel members etc. This was reneged upon and I was to receive nothing except the chance for a meeting to ask questions. They were to offer no information, simply to answer my questions. The date loomed ever near, but I couldn't let myself believe it was actually going to happen, it had been postponed so many times. Preparing myself for each date, only to find it had been changed – again, was emotionally and mentally draining.

The Hearing
Finally the day of the Hearing arrived – April 5th; well over seven months after I had made the original complaint. My advocate had requested a meeting a few days before to enable us to ask questions about the process on that day. I had no idea what to expect and couldn't have prepared myself for how it was to affect me emotionally.

I was so anxious as I waited with my Advocate to be called in. I was very glad she was there. Walking into that room was like walking into the lion's den. I was on one side of the table and they were all opposite – perhaps it felt more like facing a firing squad? There were five of them, plus John, who sat with his head down, for the duration of my statement. As I struggled to read through the nine pages, I looked across at John a couple of times. As painful as it would be; I wanted eye contact with him, force him to face me as I recounted what had happened between us. Getting to the end of the statement was the emotional equivalent to finishing a marathon. I wanted to scrunch myself up as small as possible to save myself from falling apart. I had to endure questions from the panel, it was nerve wracking as I had no idea what they were going to ask. It was a horrible experience, but I was prepared to put myself through it as I knew now that what he did was serious abuse and I couldn't bear the thought of anyone else having been taken in by him.

Needless to say, I did fall apart as soon as I left the room. I'd got through it but at great cost emotionally. I felt exposed and vulnerable – I'd attended many meetings as the service user rep, with three of the panel members where we'd all sit around a table, but this had been awful – sitting across the room with them all lined up while I read out my very personal, intimate details of what John had done to me.

I couldn't imagine how I'd ever face any of them again because they would have these images of me – or more likely opinions of me, as I didn't really expect them to believe what I'd said. They would all have been aware of the label stuck on me of 'Borderline Personality Disorder,' and that alone could quite easily cause them to make judgements about me.

The only tiny bit of hope that I had about being believed was the fact that I was well known in my service user work and had built a good reputation for myself in my role as the Chair of the User Forum. I was hopefully seen as a person of integrity, but also, I kept thinking that surely they would see I couldn't possibly be making up something like that. I knew that what had happened had really happened, but I also felt that everything was stacked against me; I was just the patient and here I was, faced with an internal investigation lead by people who worked in the same place as John, who had given me no confidence so far of the process being fair and transparent.

The wait for the outcome was going to be agonising.

I had been told I would be informed simply of the outcome of the hearing and that no detail about why or how the decision had been reached. I was angry about that and it further damaged my faith in the system.

However, I was to receive a phone call requesting that I go into the Hospital to be told, face to face, of the panel's decision. I was told that the meeting was the concluding part of the disciplinary process, but that it was unusual to have such a meeting. It was the same room again which brought back the memories of the hearing. It was all the same people again, apart from John and his union rep. The Panel Chair read from a piece of paper stating that John had agreed with the allegation that he had an 'inappropriate/unprofessional relationship with a service user' and that the allegation was upheld by the panel. Then came the part that nearly made my heart stop:

"The Panel is united in its opinion that the allegation is worthy of dismissal as it does constitute serious patient abuse."

For a couple of seconds I could not believe what I had heard – they had believed me! I had told the truth and so justice would be done, but the next sentence brought the crashing blow:

Our Disciplinary Policy requires us to take each case individually and consider all relevant circumstances. Some of the particular things we felt important were

- *John acknowledged the allegation and the stress caused to you*
- *He co-operated with the investigation*
- *The incident occurred when he was a newly qualified and inexperience nurse*
- *We believe that he initiated meetings in his desire to help*
- *On consideration of all the evidence and subsequent clinical practice, we do not believe he now poses a risk to female service users.*

I was told that he had received a final written warning and that as the allegation constituted patient abuse, it would remain on his file indefinitely.

Any thoughts of relief at being believed were overshadowed by anger and utter disbelief. I was also told that there were other reasons why he was not dismissed but they were not for discussion.

I was so much in shock that I couldn't process my thoughts and feelings. I did resort to self-harm once or twice as this had been my familiar way of coping with intolerable emotional states.

Over time I was certainly able to acknowledge my anger – oh, so people who have done something very serious are allowed to get away with it if they co-operate with the investigation? So it's OK as well if they hold their hands up (to some of it) and say they acknowledge that it had been stressful to the victim? Well that's OK then; let's use that same ridiculous reasoning for paedophiles. Would a teacher simply get a warning if they'd abused a child, because they were newly qualified and inexperienced? What complete nonsense! John was to continue to work with vulnerable people – like me – who were in hospital at their lowest ebb and would welcome someone who appeared kind and concerned about their needs. I felt like marching through the hospital declaring that John was an abuser so every body would know THE TRUTH!

How could the Trust justify their actions? How could they continue to boast their 'three star status' when they employed known abusers? How on earth could they smugly trot out their Mission Statement declaring that they sought to provide services that they or any member of their family would be happy to receive? Lying bastards – I had sat in two meetings, where in one the medical director said, "How many of us would want any of our family to stay in a place like this hospital?" In the other meeting, one of the managers said, "We'd never dream of sending any of our relatives there."

No, I wouldn't now. What had been to me a place of safety, where I had hoped to get help with my mental health problems, had become a place of fear and mistrust. I wanted to ask the chair of that panel how he'd feel if his wife was admitted to the hospital and was being 'nursed' by John. Would he be comfortable with that, would he reiterate his comment at the meeting that he did not believe John posed a risk to female patients? I don't think so.

Being newly qualified was the least of all the excuses that were justifiable in my eyes. How could there ever be any doubt that getting involved in a 'private' relationship with sexual contact, with ANY patient is wrong? It is the responsibility for the professional to adhere to professional boundaries and follow their organisation's code of conduct.

How was I going to move on from this? The suicidal thoughts started to resurface. . . I felt bitterly let down by the Trust. ('Trust' – that's a joke.)

The NMC Case
Following the Disciplinary process, I was to learn that the case had to be drawn to the attention of the Nursing and Midwifery Council (NMC) due to the nature and seriousness of it. So there began 'Investigation 2' - by the NMC this time.

Again I didn't know what to expect in terms of how long it would take and who would be involved and so on. I guess my willingness to keep going with it was based on the hope that this time, those investigating John's 'Fitness to Practice' would be objective and I would not be giving any evidence to a panel of familiar faces.

As I write my story I am one year and nine months on from the date of the case being referred to the NMC. I have endured lengthy phone calls by the Case Officer, asking me lots of detailed and personal questions to gather yet more evidence as part of his investigation. I have been constantly baffled by correspondence from the NMC about such things as the 'CCC,' (Conduct and Competence Committee) Interim order hearings, Investigating Committees, CCC Hearings and so on. It is true to say that I would not have been able to get this far without the support of the Advocacy Service. I know that I'd have given up a long time ago; such is the pressure of enduring a drawn out investigation.

The Conduct and Competence Committee decided there was a case to answer and that a Hearing would be held. The thought of putting myself through this was daunting to say the least, but it was something I needed to do as part of my own journey and with the hope that there would be a different outcome than the Employment Hearing.

The NMC originally hoped that the Hearing would take place 'in the autumn,' then it was moved to 'before the end of the year.' We are now a month into the New Year with news that there can be no time scale set due to the number of cases that have to be heard. We know that it won't be before April, but beyond that, who knows?

The Hearing is just another stage – I don't know if I will be able to 'move on' beyond the Hearing. I'm emotionally exhausted by the sheer length of time I have endured this. I *have* moved – from the abuse, to the prison of the 'Secret Years,' then out into 'Breaking the Silence,' each stage chipping away at the hold John has had on me for so long. I still feel under his power in a strange way. Just seeing him at a distance or being in the same building as him or hearing his name still has a profound effect on me emotionally. Will it take him being struck off to free me from the strangleholds? But what if he isn't and continues to work? More probably it will mean a less tangible but far more significant thing to happen: a deep inner process that acknowledges the abuse, works through the pain, anguish and self loathing and longs to no longer to be the victim.

John was very clever in outwardly appearing to care and be involved in my recovery, but in reality he was growing and nurturing a dangerous dependence, which falsely led me to think that I was safe. The experience damaged me: destroying what fragile confidence I had in myself, intensifying my fear of men and cultivating my hatred of my physical self.

Hope for the Future

The journey to freedom is proving to be long and painful, but the secret is to be well equipped. I get tired and fall down but friends pick me up. I can't read the directions for the next part of the complaints procedure, but the advocates explain them to me. I think I'm the only one, but then I speak to others. I break down in the darkness of my solitude, but then I reach out and my Faith, My God, is there in Scriptures and spiritual songs.

I sometimes feel as if one day it will all prove to be too much and I'll give up. Ten whole years of my life have been held back by John and the effect of the abuse. I feel scared at the thought of the next big step of the NMC Hearing, but I will get through it – I must – I won't let him destroy me completely.

It is still very hard to engage in service user activities with the Trust and at the same Hospital. I'm often asked why I put myself through it – part of me wants to continue with the work I've been doing, especially the training, and part of me does not want to 'go away quietly.' If I'm honest with myself, I'm still angry with the Trust's decision to keep John working at the hospital. I feel vulnerable every time I'm there, and of course, if I became ill and needed admission there is no other option locally. (Unless I could afford private care!)

I have to live in the hope and determination that I would never need inpatient care, as it would be a nightmare and feel very unsafe. I still can't believe that the Trust chose to act in favour of the professional who they themselves had found guilty of gross professional misconduct. I doubt if I will ever understand or be able to accept that.

I know it's a cliché, but life does go on. I've survived so far and have been able to recognise changes in myself. The most significant step forward is I no longer blame myself for what happened. When those strong voices of doubt whisper to me, 'you encouraged him; you should never have met him outside the hospital . . . ' etc. I have to tell myself over and over again – *he was the professional and had responsibility not to overstep the boundaries.*

Broken Boundaries

This experience of abuse still has the potential to destroy me, but I hope it won't. I hold fast to the things I have gathered so far on my journey: the gift of special friends who accept me and are there for me, courage to speak up and make a stand for truth, a gradual realisation that there is no reason for me to punish myself anymore and most of all, *hope* - that this bruised and damaged soul can *and will* be healed.

Post script

Five months on from writing this, the NMC Hearing finally took place. It was scheduled to be a two-day hearing in London. On day one, I was questioned by my Solicitor to establish the facts and then cross-examined by John's solicitor. The five panel members also questioned me. This took over five hours, with a short lunch break and brief adjournment. It was a gruelling and emotionally draining day. John was in the room the whole time. It was so hard.

On day two, I listened to John being questioned and was deeply distressed listening to his version of events. I cried many times during this - just hearing his voice was upsetting.

The panel took over two hours to deliberate. There were two serious differences in our statements. John said that sexual contact only happened once and then he stopped it straight away, and he denied voicing his desire to cut me all over.

After two long days, it was an agonising wait to hear the outcome. I held no hope that all the allegations would be upheld because it would be difficult to prove 'beyond reasonable doubt' that what I said was true.

No one could have imagined the decision of the panel. All the allegations were upheld – they believed everything I said. I was described as the 'most reliable witness.'

Unfortunately we ran out of time to bring the process to an end. I face another two months' wait to return to London for the sanctioning stage.

However I have had a fair and objective hearing this time. I faced John, I told the truth, I have been heard and believed – this long journey is nearly over and then I can begin the rest of my life.

2

Michele Matheson

It is six years almost to the day since I last saw the man whom I could never imagine living without, my *raison d'etre*, the point of my being. There was a time when I could hardly bear to go twenty-four hours without seeing him, when nothing mattered except him. I could not have imagined surviving so long without him and yet here I am, still alive and kicking. Everything and everyone, my family, my children, were eclipsed by my intense need of him. I have battled to justify, to make sense of what has happened to me, for nearly two decades, and know I have to live with the consequences until the day I die. Who else is there to take responsibility for the effect it has had, specifically on my children? Certainly not him.

My involvement with him began after a period of debilitating ill health. In 1986 I had a full hysterectomy, just before my thirty-seventh birthday. The surgeon punctured my bladder and vagina and three months later I needed major surgery again to repair the damage. This totalled five abdominal operations to date. I never really seemed to pick up after this and in the autumn of 1987 was found to have an under-active thyroid and extremely low levels of oestrogen in my system. I also had a brain scan, as there was some concern that I may have had an enlarged pituitary gland; luckily this was not the case.

Being at such low ebb brought to the surface childhood issues with my mother (who had died when I was 23 years old). My GP suggested I see Dr L, a psychiatrist whose particular interest was in psychotherapy, and, although I was not really keen to do so, I agreed to see him. By the time of my first appointment in February 1988, I had begun to feel better physically and stronger emotionally. I was now taking Thyroxine with an increased level of oestrogen replacement, but I decided to see him as I knew that the unhappy feelings about my childhood and subsequent lack of self-esteem and self-worth were definitely having an adverse effect on my life. I had been through some difficult times and I saw this as a last chance to really try and sort things out for myself, with someone whom I hoped would be able to work with me towards a better sense of myself.

The first time I went to see him, in February 1988; I talked about my mother, the things that had happened to me and how I was feeling. I cried, and remember him sitting there and just looking at me. But he seemed to think that we could work on these issues and I went away encouraged. Over the next few meetings he was very easy in his attitude to me and I found that very emotionally seductive. My sessions with him seemed quickly to become quite intense and I was rather frightened and confused by this. I felt a strong emotional connection with him and the implicit promise that perhaps this person really could `help make everything all right'. He had a very powerful presence and personality and talked to me, I felt, more as a man to a woman than a doctor to a patient.

After the first few appointments, he began to refer to the 'sexual tension between us'. I felt astonished by what he had said, but I was like a rabbit caught within blinding headlights. I was uneasy, but in a childlike way also excited by being so very special to a person such as him. I was very confused, experiencing feelings that I had not felt before. I can only describe it as like being caught up in an emotional earthquake.

He paid me a lot of attention and gave me a cassette of songs that he had put together with me in mind, telling me, "Don't tell your husband". No one had ever done that before and I felt so special and so wonderful. My need for him began to dominate my life and I was totally taken over by him.

During the first two months of meeting him, I was swept up in something quite out of my control. I adored and worshipped him; he was the most wonderful person I had ever met. His office was like a little haven, there was nobody else in the world but the two of us and he treated me as if I was a beautiful, special being. I felt a chasm in my very soul opening up to him, it was as if he was the only person ever to have recognised the real me. He understood how I felt, the way I gave no concern to my own feelings because they were unimportant. He listened to me as I talked about myself and seemed to be very responsive to me. I told him of my liking for art and about the poetry that moved me.

He encouraged me to write my own poetry, telling me that my intensity excited him, that I was beautiful and he had never felt like this before. In meeting me he had found the other half of himself, it was like looking in a mirror. When he told me, "I needed to be touched" I quite literally felt a physical shift at the very centre of myself and something just melting. He led me to open myself up to him and after the first time he kissed me, I was lost.

I had never felt so lovely and so wonderful. Even now, as I write, I can still remember that feeling and my complete connection with him. I was the other half of him and we would merge and be one forever. I thought that he would always put me first and would never let me down, that nothing and no one mattered to him as much as me. I could not bear to be away from him, I yearned for him all the time. I loved him, I felt protective of him when he told me sad things about his own life – how could I not? He said things were very difficult for him at work, he had so much responsibility, and that his wife just took him for granted. With me he felt alive for the first time. When he wanted to have sex with me, how could I turn away?

Two months after we met he took me to his home (his wife was away) and had sex with me. I knew that what I was doing was wrong, but seemed to have no control over what was happening. It took a glass of wine to relax me sufficiently to go ahead with it. There was a passion there, and after all that he had engendered in me how could this not happen – I thought we loved each other. But something in me was uncomfortable and it did not seem right to take my clothes off in front of this man. I had been married to my husband for nineteen faithful years and we had two wonderful children whom we both loved very dearly. I was so torn.

Afterwards I could not look him in the face.

Broken Boundaries

When I arrived home, I felt so ashamed, so guilty, so wicked, so dirty. I jumped straight into the bath and swore to myself never see him again. I had broken my marriage vows and betrayed my family, and I felt despicable. I was torn in two, with my feelings for them and my feelings for him. But within a few days he was phoning me and again, I seemed powerless to resist. It was as if he could tap into the heart of my neediness, absorb it into himself and make me feel completely safe and loved for the first time in my life. It was, quite literally, an irresistible feeling and all I wanted was to be with him. I could not envisage life without him. It was a terrible situation to be in.

The next few weeks were awful. Living a lie was not something that came naturally to me and I felt that I had lost myself. I had also lost the support that I had gone to him for, as our relationship had shifted into something entirely different. Then out of the blue he told his wife he was "having an affair with a patient". He told me without any consultation (as one would in an equal, adult relationship) and that he had had to tell her, as he felt so bad about his family. I was then put in the position of feeling that I should tell my husband I had "fallen in love" – it seemed the more honourable thing to do. He then moved out of his home and I felt I should leave mine. The life that I had lived up until then, as a wife and loving mother, was blown apart and the only thing that kept me going was the certainty of our 'love'. That seems so pathetic now, but at the time was overwhelming and even now I feel disloyal to him writing this.

I truly believed we loved one another overwhelmingly. He told me this had never happened with a patient before; he had never been unfaithful to his wife. I believed him, but there have been subsequent rumours that I have heard since. I would feel jealous and possessive about his relationships with other vulnerable female patients who obviously thought he was wonderful too. There was definitely something about him that made him attractive to vulnerable women. What made me different from them – why me? Why had I been chosen – was it something I did, was I really that lovable, that wonderful?

He managed to hang on to his job by saying that I was not a patient when we began our 'affair' and destroyed what few notes he had written about me. Amazingly, shamefully, he got away with it. When I asked him if he had not thought out the consequences of what had happened between us, he said he had not. I remember feeling quite shocked, this was not what I expected of this superhuman person, who had the answers to everything. I asked him why he had done it and he told me that he had been having such a hard time at work he felt he deserved something nice. It just goes to show how in thrall I was that on hearing I was 'something nice to perk up his life' I just sat there. He did not mean it, I was sure. I knew he loved me.

I went along with all that he said and did as if I were a child. All the feelings that had erupted in me before we had sex, were still there and just as powerful. But I had been catapulted from being someone who was at the time very vulnerable and seeking help, to having to be an adult woman trying to conduct a relationship and do the best I could by my family. It was a long time before I recognised the wrongness of this.

I cannot over-emphasize the devastating effect all this had on my husband and children. I think they could not recognise the person they had known – a family orientated wife and mother. It was as if an alien had invaded my being and I was speaking and behaving in ways that were just not me. It is difficult after these years to understand the intensity of my feelings for him and the total subjugation of my will to his. My daughter tells me that it was not love I felt, but need and I am sure she is right. But at the time I felt my loyalty had shifted to him and that is a terrible thing to say and way to feel.

He took on a dingy little flat and we moved in there, supposedly until we could get somewhere with extra room so the children could stay. I also had to get a part time job as he said he could not afford to support me as well as his family, but I didn't mind that. It was all such hard work and somehow the whole situation did not feel right, like living in some weird dream that was happening to someone else. I cooked the sort of meals he liked - vegetarian at that time - worked, saw what I could of my family while always putting him first. It was exhausting, but I could do nothing else. The time that we spent together, under 'normal' circumstances, was not right, but I adored him and my dependency on him was total.

It quickly evolved, now we were in the 'real world', that he did not want me to have much to do with my children and he certainly didn't want them around him, particularly my son, who was only 9 at the time, whom he wanted to shut out completely. This was so very difficult, I know my family could not understand what was happening and I am still tormented by the shame of it all. It became apparent that what he wanted was a mirror image of himself, someone who never had thoughts or ideas that would contradict his own, someone who adored him unquestioningly. Essentially he was using me to make himself feel omnipotent and the person who was me was actually not that important, although it was a number of years before I recognised this fact.

Broken Boundaries

So, when I tried to deal on a practical level with my family's needs, this began to cause dissent. In fact, this was when I first saw the unpleasant and totally selfish side of him. There were times when his cruelty was astounding. But I was like a child in this relationship, and like an abused child I did all I could to make him happy. Of course I know now that I could never do that.

Then after a couple of months he told me out of the blue that he could not live without his family – it "hurt him too much" - and was going home. One day I arrived back at the flat after work to find he had stripped it of everything that was his and gone, with absolutely no concern for me or what I would do.

It is hard to describe the feeling of total and utter abandonment, like nothing I had ever felt before. It was November 1988, dark and cold and I had no idea what on earth I was going to do, literally like an abandoned small child. How could he take me out of my family and then walk out with no care for what would become of me? I think in spite of his own feelings my husband felt sorry for me, that I had been caught up in something that was not right and he asked me to return home. I did, for him, my poor son and my daughter who was by now at university, although I felt I had so little to give them.

It was so difficult, I could not stop longing for him and needing him, it dominated my life. I had given him all of me and he had abandoned me. I was stick thin and had great difficulty sleeping. I tried to cope at home, but they knew how unhappy I was and that Christmas was so sad for all of us. I had lost myself and my children had lost their mother. The only relief that I could find was in writing. I wrote many poems through all this, it was a way of channelling the terrible sense of loss, the pain and the longing I had inside myself. It is a dreadful thing to be in such thrall to another human being, for them to have such control over you. I could not see this at the time, it has taken years of hard work and striving to try to get myself together again.

After no contact for two months or so, he phoned me. He had kept the little flat going, goodness knows why, and he now wanted to "sort things out". We met there one lunchtime and it began again. Looking back, everything was always about him, his feelings and what he wanted. He was so wrapped up in himself and how he was suffering. Quite quickly after he first had sex with me, the caring role swung around from him to me and that is how it basically stayed, to the detriment of my own, or anyone else's, feelings and needs. I ended up trying to help him, his hurts and what he had been going through and that took precedence over all else.

Needless to say, I could not continue at home with all this going on, he said again that he wanted to be with me and we moved back into the flat after a few months. In February 1990 he told me he wanted to leave again, the day before I was to start a new job. Then he went. I stayed on in this awful little flat, the job was not a suitable one for me and my father was dying. Meanwhile, he had gone on a holiday by himself, he said, because he could not cope with his feelings of me being someone else's wife and told me to "separate yourself from your husband and then we will see".

We duly went through the courts and obtained a legal separation. It was so sad, and seemed so wrong somehow. I think both of us felt rather bewildered by what was happening and the fact it should never have happened like this at all. I felt so overwhelmingly alone.

Needless to say, his promised divorce did not materialise.

In April 1990 my father died. Even then, his feelings took precedence over mine or those of my family and he would not give me the support and comfort that anyone would have expected at that time. I felt I could not deal properly with my father's death, for myself or my family as he would always want something from me. I was caught in the middle and very alone. I had adored my father - it was a very black time.

In the autumn, he told me he was going to stop paying the rent on the flat and I would either have to take it over myself or move out. I moved between flats until April 1991, when he moved away from the area to a new job, effectively abandoning his family as well as me. He told me he wanted to be by himself, and because I always put his feelings before my own, I respected his need. This was a very bad time for me. Again, the feelings of abandonment were very intense, a very close friend was dying of cancer, I was beginning another job and also living somewhere new. That summer was a time of great grief for me. I felt that I had lost so much. I do not know how I managed to carry on at that time.

All through this my family were trying to survive as well. I was so little use to them as I was completely taken up with him and what he needed and wanted. This is what makes me feel angry – he abandoned me and I abandoned them. I will never lose this feeling of shame at the wrong that I felt I did.

Broken Boundaries

Then, in the autumn, I heard that he was getting back with his wife. After telling me he could not be with me because he just had to be on his own, this felt such a betrayal. I always believed everything that he told me, every single word, because I trusted him completely. To think that he might lie to me was inconceivable. How naïve. Of course, I can see that to have a woman who behaves emotionally like a child with you is impossible, but then, I had not asked to be put in that situation. I was exhausted, grief stricken and guilt ridden. I pretty well broke down at this stage, it had all become too much for me to deal with.

I moved to London to be with my daughter and take up a place at college that I had been offered. Within a few months he had tracked me down and made contact again. Apparently he and his wife were not getting back together, he missed me, could not stop thinking about me and wanted to see me.

Again, my need for him was overwhelming. I had never felt about anyone as I felt about him. Again, he was caught up in how sad, bad, et cetera he felt and again, I was in the role of rescuer. We started up again, although I was not allowed to tell anyone about this and we would only see each other when it suited him, usually for sex. My daughter knew of course, which was rather compromising for her. Still we were a destroyed family seemingly controlled by him and what he wanted. I despised myself for how I felt.

I spent two years in London, it was a very unhappy time in my life. I worked really hard, gained a Diploma in the course I was taking, tried to do the best I could by my son and retain whatever sanity I could under the circumstances. He had been vitriolic in his rejection and total lack of concern for my son.

In 1993 my daughter wanted to move in with her boyfriend and I needed to move on, again. He grudgingly told me I could stay with him until I had sorted myself out. So, I moved again, but this time he seemed to quite enjoy me being around and I was allowed to stay. But I was not allowed to tell anyone.

So began a few years together, seemingly as a couple. But nothing had really changed. It still was not right somehow – how could it ever be? He refused to have anything to do with my son; I had to deal with that on a separate basis. When we were initially looking for somewhere to live, we viewed one house with a telephone booth right outside on the street. He favoured this one, because I could use that to telephone my son and not have to use "his" phone or give out the home number, although of course his family were allowed to have it.

It was when I was in London that I first came across Peter Rutter's book 'Sex in the Forbidden Zone'. Reading it was a revelation for me, I could not believe that I was reading exactly what had happened to me. All the feelings I had experienced were written in this book! This was the beginning for me of not feeling as if it was all my fault, but it was a very confusing situation to be in while we were living together as a 'normal couple'. In retrospect it is much easier to see how we could never really have been a normal couple because of the power imbalance. After some time, I plucked up courage and showed him Peter Rutter's book and asked him to read through so that he could understand how I felt, which he did. I had marked out many passages which I felt referred to me and he took all this on board. Amazingly none of this seemed to have occurred to him before.

For a while after things improved and he was much kinder and more considerate of my feelings, but of course it could not last. We had rows about the children; he refused to tell his children we were together. I felt they had a right to know and to visit their father. If we were together then we had to include his and my children in our lives; after all, we were supposed to be the adults. Eventually he did agree that it was cruel to shut them all out and they began to visit. I gave his children lots of time and space to be with their father when they were with us and to get on with them as well as possible, although I think they always blamed me for what happened. It is so sad that they are unable to see it as it really was. My son was always suspicious of him and found him rather threatening; I tried very hard to care for him in all this.

Through all this I was working and trying to feel 'normal'. That must sound really silly, and it is only easier to see now in retrospect. In many ways I am finding writing about this period the most difficult, because I was so torn between us being a normal couple and the fact that I had been used. I felt like a fraud, that everyone would find out that I had been a 'patient', that I was living a life that was not my life. The pain I felt about my family was ongoing, although I am sure they just thought that I was having a great time and did not care about them. It was a terrible situation to be in, but I just did not know what else to do. I had given up everything for him, if I was not with him, then what would I do?

The disparity between us caused friction. I told him that I thought marriage would equal things between us. He told me (he was still not yet divorced) that although he loved me, he would never marry again and allow another woman access to his money. This was in spite of me committing what money I had into our home, as he did not have the ready cash. I respected his feelings, as ever. During this time my own divorce became finalised, which was very painful as it did not actually feel like a conscious decision made between my husband and myself, rather something that had been engineered. I was very upset. Soon after our divorce, my ex-husband re-married, but this relationship was not to be a lasting one for him.

In 1998 we moved again, for a new job opportunity for him. I was becoming increasingly depressed and knew in my heart that this was not really for me. My son had been having problems with alcohol and drug taking and my daughter had some quite demanding things going on in her life. I was exhausted with trying to work, move to a new area and do what I could to support my family. We found another home and I finally gave up work, seemingly with his blessing and encouragement so that I could give more time to my children and hopefully find something for myself that I would find fulfilling. Thus, I was able to spend a lot of time that year with my children.

During this time he told me he had "fallen out of love with me". He was fed up with my children and their problems and "wanted to be on his own". Once more all the feelings of being rejected and abandoned flooded back. If it had been a 'normal' relationship, we could have separated and gone our own ways, despite the pain. It would have been difficult, but no different to what lots of other couples do. We talked and I thought we were going to try and resolve things.

Through the following winter my son became increasingly ill, and I had to spend much time travelling and trying to help sort things out for him.

The eighteen months from the summer of 1999 were very bad. I had been through several periods in my 'relationship' with him that had been incredibly painful and this last one was extremely difficult. He was telling me he no longer loved me and that I had to move out of our home, otherwise he would stop paying the mortgage. When I said I could not possibly take this on I was told to just go. Should I stick a pin in the map and go there? He did not care. I was in a strange part of the country, with no one to turn to. I did not know where to go and felt totally lost. My parents were dead, my sister and daughter both lived overseas and the people from my previous life were effectively lost to me. I had no idea what I was to do.

Michele Matheson

One day when sorting out the laundry, I spotted something pink on his shirt collar. My initial reaction was that this was lipstick and I was distraught. It took me ages to pluck up courage to mention it and his explanation was that he had been eating tomato at lunch and it had dropped off his fork! It seems risible now. I did ask him if there was someone else, but he would look me straight in the eye and say no. He kept telling me that he just wanted to be on his own. Through all this time also I was supporting him as he went through his own long and difficult divorce – I had thought once that was finalised, then we could have had our own life.

I cannot actually recall too much of what happened through the year 2000. I know it was bleak and lonely, we both continued to live in our house and he would go away increasingly for work. My gut feeling told me there was someone else, but he always denied it and because the whole basis of our relationship had begun on total trust (I thought), I believed him.

Throughout this year I was trying to come to terms with the possibility of losing him and the practicality of finding somewhere else to live. It was very hard as I was still living in the house, but he was just emotionally detached from me and could be extremely cruel in his behaviour towards me and in the things that he said. His view seemed to be that the relationship did not work for him and so I had to go, but added that the sex had been "quite literally, mind blowing".

I felt so used. What about all those feelings, all the things he said to me? Did it just boil down to the fact he wanted some excitement in his life and I turned up at the right time, to provide him with "mind blowing" sex? I had given him my very soul. Some years ago I wrote the following:

You took possession of my heart and shattered it
You took possession of my body and made it your own
You took possession of my soul and raped it
You took possession of my mind and nearly destroyed it

I felt like a small, grubby, discarded child. The way he treated me was very abusive and I suppose as in all abusive situations, how you are treated and how you feel, become the norm. Gradually my own sense of self worth and self-esteem, always rocky, sank lower and lower. I kept myself busy with the normal day to day things that needed to be done, solely to retain my sanity, and the few people I could talk to about it on the phone were always there for me and incredibly supportive.

Broken Boundaries

Deciding where to move to next was difficult. I could not go back to the place where I had been born and lived during my married life and yet I was so frightened at the thought of moving, alone, to an unknown place. I knew that I was just not strong enough emotionally to be able to do it. Eventually I decided to check out the town where I now live, and there were just two things on which I based my choice. I wanted to be near the sea again and I also had a dear friend who lived here and who was incredibly supportive. So in the autumn of 2000 I came here and started to look around at the possibilities.

When I returned home I began to put in place the arrangements I would need to make. Throughout all this I had no help from him, or even any interest, just rejection and emotional abuse. I had to be very strong. He would not allow me to tell his family that we were breaking up and I was moving. I can see now that was just cowardice on his part and his usual way of being in total control, regardless of me or my feelings. We had to get through Christmas with his family and the only way I could do this was by just accepting that I could do nothing to change what was happening in the house. Going against his decisions would destroy me and I would not be able to function.

When I left in the New Year, with just what I could pack in a few bags, he was very upset. Again, he was only ever really tuned in to his own feelings. I do not know how I got through that day. As he was "so upset", he told me that we would sort out our mutual possessions at a later date. Subsequently this was again sorted out in his way. I was not able to return to go through everything, as he "could not cope with seeing me again". What I received was what he had decided he did not want. There was no point in arguing about it, he would always win.

When I arrived in my new town I was not in a good way. I had sorted out a flat in which to stay temporarily and was not sure if I would be able to survive this time. I decided to write a diary, something I had done previously when he had moved away from our area to a new job. I recorded, ironically, that here I was doing this all over again ten years on, emotionally destroyed and having to start all over again. I had never felt so alone.

It was during my final months with him that I had first contacted WITNESS, (POPAN at the time), feeling incredibly disloyal to him in doing so. The person there that I spoke to was very supportive and when I arrived in my new place kept in regular contact to help me and give me a lifeline at such a very difficult time and I have never forgotten that.

Michele Matheson

This was probably the lowest time of all the years since I had met him, and I had been through some lows. The weather was cold and wet and I hid under my duvet, utterly destroyed by all that had happened and all that I had lost. I missed him so much and could not understand how someone who had taken me over so totally could now abandon me to this. There must have been something about me, about how I had related to him that made him do what he had done. Surely I would not have gone along with it if there were not some dreadful flaw in me.

I had never, ever felt so alone and my thoughts turned seriously to suicide. The few people I had left that were close to me were exhausted by my desperate unhappiness and their inability to deal with it. My son was deteriorating, with his father trying to cope with him. I felt I had let down my family completely and was a worthless and disgusting human being. The only thing to do was to end it all.

I had lost count of the number of soulless flats I had lived in over the years, the number of times I had felt alone and abandoned, hurt and confused at how I found myself living. I had lost my home, my family and brought down on my head scorn and contempt from the people among whom I lived. I had spent years suffering inside for what I had done to my husband and especially my children. I could never regain the time I had lost with them and they would always have to live with feeling abandoned in turn. I had lost the one person in whom I had invested my very soul. I had cried more tears than it seemed possible to cry, over and over and over again.

I had repeatedly put his needs and what he wanted before my own or anyone else's. I had done everything that he had demanded of me, to the detriment of my own self. I had listened to him telling me that he saw himself as a kind and helpful human being who would do anything for anyone and I felt confused and uncertain about myself, as in large part this was not really my experience of him.

When we were with other people he was funny, witty and clever, but he was also cruel and selfish. I had seen him at work, where everyone thought he was marvellous, so empathic with the patients, so charismatic, so clever, so much in charge. At home, he would be scathing and rejecting, saying things about me that made me feel less than a piece of dirt on his shoe and then walking away, leaving me to wither up inside myself. Everything was always about him.

So why didn't I kill myself? My children. Bloody mindedness.

Broken Boundaries

I thought that a screwed up mother was probably better than no mother at all, that to kill myself would be to abandon them all over again.

I thought, why should I kill myself because of what he did – then he really would have won.

And so I chose life.

That must have been a kind of turning point for me, but the rawness, loneliness, pain and fear were intense. And I missed him, still found myself in the role of his carer on the odd occasion we spoke on the phone to sort out the practicalities, and each time I felt so vulnerable afterwards. Once everything was finalised, I did not hear from him again.

In the autumn of that year, 2001, I heard that another woman had moved into what was our home, and had been staying there soon after I had gone. The strongest feeling I had was one of betrayal. He had gone on so much about wanting to be on his own and never wanting to marry again. I had always put his feelings above my own, and he had been lying. There had been someone else all along.

By this time I was working and making some sort of life for myself here. The relationship with my daughter was on a more even keel, but my son was increasingly unwell. This has been an ongoing and extremely painful situation to deal with, especially under the circumstances. I made a conscious effort to tell a few select people about what had happened to me, but it was very difficult as I still carry so much shame. But it is a major part of my life and so how could I relate to new friends if they had no knowledge of what has made me? In some ways I wish I had not revealed such a painful part of my life, but why should *I* feel shamed and secretive?

The next piece of news I received was that he had married the woman who had moved in. This was very, very hard for me to accept. After all he had said, after all the support and care I had given him and his feelings, after I had put myself on the back burner to make him happy, it was all a sham. He had lied to me, spun me a line, taken me for a ride. I felt so stupid, so worthless, so utterly rejected. It took me months to come to terms with that piece of news. How could he do this, after all he had said to me? Even now, it still hurts when I think of it.

He has only ever thought of himself, only ever done what he wanted to do for himself. It is extremely hard for me not to be eaten up with bitterness. That he could walk over other people the way he has done, with no sense of guilt and no conscience is astounding. But the feelings I had for him were overwhelming and still I am torn between the two.

It is six years since I last saw him and I have had many dreams about him, nearly always set in what was our home.

I live day to day as best I can. My son now lives in the same town as me and is in the care of the mental health services. I give much time and effort in trying to improve his life and care, but it is exhausting, emotionally and physically. Sometimes I think this is my legacy for being so wicked, even if intellectually I can see that this is not logical. His life was ruined, in large part, by me leaving and because of that I will never have peace of mind.

I feel very isolated as I do not think I will ever be able to have a loving relationship. I got it all so wrong with him, and feel that I do not know what love is. What I thought was love was really a sham. If that felt so strong and right, but was not, then my judgement is flawed. It would be very difficult for me to let another man close to me emotionally again and that makes me feel very lonely.

Sometimes I wonder how it would be if we met again, there is so much I would like to ask him. But I know it would open me up all over again, I would revert to a child emotionally and I do not think I could survive those feelings again. I still long for him at times, although I know it is not him that I long for, rather the promise I felt when I first knew him. That little piece of me will forever be raw, and that is a very lonely feeling. All that he has put me through has added to the issues I first took to him.

I can see, objectively, that I must be fairly strong to have made a reasonable life for myself. I have a few people whom I know genuinely care for me, in spite of how I feel about myself underneath, some of whom know what has happened to me. Much of the time I feel as if I am acting out a life, but what else can I do? And there are good things, times when I feel more real. The searing longing has abated somewhat, but I know it will never really leave me.

When I told a friend that I was writing this, she said that at least I would be writing from the heart. Without thought I replied "I will be writing from the head, my heart is frozen", and that is true.

3

Louisa Street

My story is about emotional abuse. Not sexual, emotional - and like other victims of emotional abuse, it's very hard for me to write about and hard to get across how damaging it was. You can only understand the impact on me if you accept that because of my therapist's influence over me, I accepted everything he said as literally true. Someone once told me, "If your therapist says the sky is green, you see a green sky or you feel guilty". He, like other therapists in a transference situation, was in a position to tell me what my reality was. This of course, is a dangerous imbalance of power, and because of his own emotional problems, which I now realise were far worse than mine, he used this power for his own gratification.

I went to see a therapist because I lacked confidence. I was about 23 at the time, and working in an office as a typist. I was bored out of my mind, and more than anything else, I wanted to go to university. However, because I lacked confidence, I had failed my O levels and couldn't get myself together to study in the evening.

He advertised hypnosis on blue and white posters all round the city. He called himself a Doctor of Psychology with a string of other letters after his name.   Only a long time afterwards, I discovered all these qualifications were fakes and he had been the subject of a few complaints to the British Medical Association (BMA).   They, typically, had warned him and then done nothing.   I just went for hypnosis.   He advertised hypnosis on posters and I just wanted a quick cure to make me more confident.   He told me that this wouldn't work and the only thing that would was analysis, which would take a long time.

He was a Freudian, and very early on he diagnosed me as suffering from "penis envy".   As I lacked confidence, I considered any ambition I had as a female to be pathological, so having a name for the pathological condition seemed to constitute a brilliant explanation.   Anyway, by then, I was "in love" with him and would have accepted anything he said.   I had read up on psychoanalysis, knew all about "transference" love.   I always knew it wasn't real love, but I soon had no control over what I felt, and became more dependent on him as the therapy proceeded.   It's difficult to explain.   I just "fell in love" with him the second time I saw him.   He seemed so much more powerful than me, a rescuer.   It just happened.   I suppose because he called himself a doctor, I assumed he had a great mind.

I managed to tell him quite early on that I was in love with him.   As I said, I had done some reading on counselling and I knew about transference. He told me it was part of the therapy process and I would have to work through it.   He said I must go into it and allow myself to feel it.   He told me I should trust him because the one thing he would never do is to end therapy with a client who was dependant.   This encouragement to experience my feelings, whether it was my love for him or my sexual feelings or my anger, to the full, without inhibition was one of the main themes all throughout the therapy.

After eight years of the therapy, I wasn't any more confident but I was more dependent on him.   If anything, I was less confident because I lived in his shadow.   I wanted to be like him.

My dependence manifested itself simply by the fact that my whole life revolved around going to see him.   I can't remember what I said to him about this, but I am sure he knew.   I think he got pleasure out of this, but we both knew it was part of the therapy situation.   Once, I told him that the first time I saw him I thought he was really ugly and he told me that was my protection against the positive feelings I now felt.

I also remember an incident where he came in wearing a really loud plaid suit. I said it was awful - after all he had told me to say the first thing that came into my head. He spent the whole of my hour trying to persuade me I really liked it but I was defending myself against this feeling.

However, when I did really experience my feelings he didn't like it. Towards the end of the therapy, I had almost a mystical experience of being united with him. I thought this was very positive, but when I told him about it, he seemed less than pleased. He didn't say anything. He just became very cold towards me. He didn't even try to interpret it, although I am quite aware this is not a unique experience and there is an interpretation. Possibly, he couldn't deal with so much closeness. My therapist friend tells me that maybe he lost interest in me because he "had" me; I was no longer a challenge.

About six months before my university finals, I cancelled two appointments because I was running out of money. I phoned his answer phone. When I came for my appointment on the third week, he told me he never got my cancellation and he had given my appointment time to someone else.

I waited about six weeks to hear from him. Remember, by now, my whole life revolved round him. When I still heard nothing, I started to get frantic. My concentration went to pieces. Then, I remembered he had always chided me for not being spontaneous and not being assertive so I thought I would go to his office when he came out for his lunch hour and ask him when my next appointment would be. I wasn't prepared for the reception I got.

His charm dropped and he flew at me. He told me I never seemed to learn anything. He told me my subconscious aggression was the reason for the answer-phone messages getting lost. As we sat in his office, I realised I wasn't going to be able to cope with this sudden break-up. By then, I'd been seeing him for eight years and I was really addicted. I said, "You must really hate me", and he said, "No" and sent me away to wait for an appointment.

Remember, everything he said, I took literally. Firstly, I couldn't stand him being annoyed with me for something that wasn't my fault. If he was angry with me, for not making progress, why didn't he talk about it before, and if he thought it wasn't worth my coming, he could have said. I was also very upset because I idealised him and I couldn't accept that he thought that my subconscious mind could interfere with the telephone lines. I thought he literally believed this and it seemed nonsense. Maybe he did believe it, but for me, it showed him as someone with very flawed thinking. But he was my saviour, the person who had deigned to rescue me from my miserable life and I couldn't bear to think he was like this.

I waited for several weeks. I found I couldn't work. My concentration had disappeared down a black hole. It was far more than anything I could control. I remember it took me one whole day to read one page of a very standard psychology paperback. I started writing him more and more desperate letters. It seemed to me, the person I had loved so much had suddenly switched off and wasn't there any more. More than anything, I keep stressing, "If you are annoyed with me, why can't we discuss it" and then, "If you don't want to see me, at least tell me". I told him over and over again in all my letters and phone calls that I didn't expect him to continue to treat me if he didn't want to. All I wanted was for him to be honest. If he was angry with me, we should be able to talk about it, and if he wanted to end therapy he should have said, not left me hanging on. What made me feel so helpless is that he didn't say anything. I heard nothing. At one point, he rang me up and accused me of being omnipotent in wanting an appointment that he didn't have. Altogether, I went three months before I saw him again.

With my exams weeks away, part of my rational mind that was still active realised I was in a bad way and that without an explanation from him I couldn't cope. I knew all about transference in psychology, I knew what was wrong with me but I still couldn't do anything about it. I wrote a letter telling him I didn't want to see him any more and I was going to Spain. I wasn't going to Spain, or anywhere else but I think by then, I knew this was all about control and I wanted him to think he couldn't control me. I was right. I got an appointment back by return.

If I thought we could now discuss things, I was wrong. The sessions were gobbledygook. I kept asking him what had happened and I thought we could have a normal conversation to sort things out, but he insisted on continuing to give a Freudian interpretation to every question I asked him.

"Why are you doing this to me?"

"The reason you want to know is because you've never sublimated your subconscious aggression".

Louisa Street

He also kept insisting I was omnipotent in wanting an appointment when there weren't any available, but I had checked - a friend of mine had rung him during this time and got an appointment within a week.

He had done serious damage to my degree chances by not seeing me. He would have known the effects of just dropping a client, yet when I asked him why he told me that wanting to know was neurotic. Again, you can only understand the impact of this if you understand that because of his influence over me, I felt compelled to accept everything he told me as literally true. Wanting to know must be a symptom of my neurosis, but if I accepted that, it would mean I had no rights whatsoever.

The four weeks I saw him were torture. It seemed like reality was being bent to whatever he wanted it to be and I couldn't find a way out.

Later on, lawyers and anyone else I asked for help treated me as an accredited loony. Because I was disbelieved before I even opened my mouth, I carefully analysed everything I said to make sure it was socially acceptable. I realised words like "torture" and "brainwashing" might seem like proof to people of my precarious mental state. But I decided that however emotive the words were, they were totally accurate and not some hysterical exaggeration. It was torture. I felt he was trying to argue me out of my core values, the very person I was. If I believed him, it wouldn't be me any more and I might as well be dead.

Anyway, I went in for my exams without revision, I did badly and got a third, but at least I passed. I wrote and cancelled any further appointments. I was still lucid enough to know he was damaging me. However, I found I couldn't stop seeing him. I tried again to get an explanation from him, but I got thrown out of his office and got a warning note from his solicitor.

This was a bad move on his part. If he had just said, "sorry", I would have accepted it. Now he had opened a new dimension.

A few months after therapy ended, I found out his qualifications had been faked. It was easy enough to do. There was a book listing qualifications in the library. (Incidentally, I would advise everyone to check on his or her therapist). Why hadn't I done it before? Then, as he claimed his degree was American, I wrote to the American Embassy and discovered there were no valid qualifications with that string of letters. Later, I actually went do see a very nice man at the BMA and learnt he was the subject of several complaints, not only for pretended qualifications but there had been an accusation (unproven) that he had been performing abortions. I met other people he had damaged. They were mostly people he had damaged by hypnosis. He gave them suggestions like, "From now on you will always be happy", and the first man I met found he couldn't react normally any more. One hypnotherapist had even gone down to warn my therapist and got thrown out, "Who the hell do you think you are?" From a social worker, I learned "Mr. ...... is a menace. He leaves people hung up in transference situations" and from a Catholic Priest I got a statement, "I have met several people who have consulted Mr. ...... None have come to any good, and some have come to positive harm".

The man who had been damaged by hypnosis had contacted a newspaper, The News of the World. I didn't know whether to do the same, but with the frightening possibility of getting my name in the paper, I contacted a lawyer and ended up suing him for misrepresentation and negligence.

I sued but got nowhere. I couldn't put my case across to my lawyer coherently. I was thinking far too slowly to deal with the rapid interaction, five minutes in a lawyer's office.

I could give a blow-by-blow account of what happened but I couldn't summarise it or explain why it was wrong, which is what I needed to do for a lawyer who didn't understand transference. It was like I could see a tree, another one, another one, but was not being able to say, "that's a forest".

Thinking slowly and not realising, it is an interesting state to be in, though I wouldn't recommend it. Although I didn't realise it at the time, what my therapist had done to me had left me intellectually damaged. I was aware that my memory wasn't functioning any more, but I was in a totally altered state of consciousness and I couldn't explain this to anyone. In particular, I was thinking too slowly to explain myself to a young, trendy lawyer, who didn't know anything about counselling or transference.

If you tell your lawyer or anyone else, "There's something wrong with my memory", the answer comes back "What's wrong with it?", but you can't reply because the answer to that question is in your memory. I would say, "I keep going upstairs to get things and come down without them", and people would reply, "I do that as well". I couldn't explain that the extent to which I was doing it was abnormal for me and that was in addition to all the other things I was forgetting. I had a serious memory problem. I couldn't access my memories or find the phrases to explain it. He would tell me something that had happened in the case and if I wasn't happy and wanted to query it I couldn't think of what I wanted to ask him until I was outside and it was too late.

Remember, at that time, 1970 or so, there were no counterbalancing arguments against the influence of a therapist. If you disagreed with your therapist, it was because you were mentally disturbed. The lawyer knew this and I was very aware of it as well. I thought, 'I can't tell him I know he thinks I'm mad, because that'll be embarrassing and he'll think I'm mad for saying it.' In fact, I later found out he told my friend who worked in his office, "She's a complete loony".

The lawyer sent me to two psychiatrists. Again, I couldn't give an account of myself in the time allowed. The first one got my five-page written account with a page missing and never noticed, so presumably he never read it. He asked, "Are you OK now" and I said, "Yes" because I didn't want him to think I was crazy and discredit my story. Then he asked again, and all I could think was "They always ask you twice to make sure you aren't lying" and I said, "Yes" again. He warned me that if I continued to sue my therapist, no other therapist would treat me.

He knew Mr. ...... had fake qualifications, but later, in his report he said anyone could practice psychoanalysis except when it came to treating schizophrenics.

He was so condescending. He told me, "They let anyone go to university nowadays" and in his report he wrote, "She must have been quite intelligent, because she had O levels at the time". I was so annoyed at this, I rejoined Mensa.

My second psychiatric report was from someone who was just totally sarcastic. Again, he wrote in his report that I was bound to keep going to psychotherapists, and if I sued, no one else would treat me. He also said, "Mr. ...... told her he wanted to end therapy." This wasn't true. In fact, I had repeatedly stressed this wasn't the case. So why had he said this? Where did he get it?

Anyway, like I said, only loonies sue their therapists and my lawyers totally messed me about. Not only did they do nothing, they messed me about doing it. Both the psychiatrists knew my therapist had fake qualifications. One of them more or less said it didn't matter. However, for both of them, I was the one who wasn't believed.

By then, I had realised there was no possible way to complain about a therapist. Somewhere along the way, the film One Flew Over the Cuckoos Nest came out and it was all true. By then, I had joined an anti-Psychiatry group (Mental Patients Union) and I stood outside the cinema handing out leaflets for the then emerging anti-Psychiatry movement. Even thinking slowly, I worked out that if patients couldn't complain then of course there would be abuse in therapy because it could flourish unchecked. But, thinking slowly, I couldn't realise why no one else could see that.

Incidentally, I now feel that the mental health of both psychiatrists and one solicitor were as questionable as my own. Of course, feeling very vulnerable at the time, I never considered that. I would say that only my barrister had effective thinking skills and the ability to base his opinions on evidence. He later became a High Court Judge.

I couldn't get across to anyone the fact that my memory didn't work. My doctor told me to write things down and I felt guilty because I couldn't do it. I thought I wasn't trying hard enough. I couldn't tell her I couldn't write everything down.

In fact, there is no compensation for a brain that doesn't work. During the days after she said that I worked out that the advice was like telling someone to take a notebook into the grave and keep notes to remind yourself what it's like to be alive. My brain wasn't working any more and I couldn't compensate by doing anything because I wouldn't remember to do it, and there was too much to write down.

I went to a student counsellor. She gave me a standard memory test, and I scored OK. I later found out it was useless for short-term memory loss. In fact, she asked me who the then Prime Minister was and I didn't know. She didn't think it odd that a recent Sociology graduate wouldn't know that. She labelled me as "attention seeking". I told myself the only way I could prove I wasn't attention seeking was not to ask for any more help, and I didn't for about 30 years. By then, I felt seeking help was damaging me as much as the original trauma.

I couldn't give a good account of myself in any interview. If I wanted to explain, I just rabbited on. I had to say everything as soon as it came into my head because I couldn't store information as memories. If the conversation went off on a tangent, I could never remember to bring it back to the main subject. In most interviews, I wanted to give a good impression, so I didn't get upset or emotional because I knew that would discredit me. But then, as I behaved cool and collected, they assumed nothing was wrong with me. I couldn't get across the fact that there was something wrong with me because I simply couldn't manage to actually say it.

If you want to know something about how I felt, try this. Imagine you are at a party and you get drunk. You are not so drunk you fall over, but you know you won't be able to drive. There are people at the party you want to impress, so you very carefully keep behaving as though you aren't drunk. You can manage it, and only you are aware that your reactions have slowed down. Then imagine you get up the next morning and you are still as drunk, and it stays like that. You can behave in such a way that no one realises it. It takes you longer to do things, but you can't tell anyone and no one knows. In my case, when I tried to tell people something was wrong, I didn't have the speed or the fluency to put my case across.

The analogy I used at the time was that it was like having an invisible arrow through your middle. You're not OK, but no one else can see it, so no one will believe you.

Then, I seemed to be in a strange world that didn't make sense any more. I was so confused I started to record the phone conversations with my lawyer. He said something, which he later said he didn't say. I couldn't understand why he said it and then said he didn't say it. I was thinking too slowly to realise he was lying.

I remember, in my barrister's office, I quoted the then popular author psychiatrist Thomas Szasz, something about the therapy industry being the modern equivalent of the medieval inquisition. Both my friend and he cut me short because they thought I was saying something embarrassing and loony, but in fact, they hadn't read the books and I couldn't explain. Thomas Szasz said the client is always in the wrong, just as the medieval witch was in the wrong in front of the inquisition. If you complain they simply use that as further proof of your wrongdoing.

My therapist had kept a couple of pages of the dreams I had written down whilst in therapy and he sent them to my lawyer. Only years later, I realised he was trying to pass them off as statements by me. There was something in them about birds flying through my living room. Again, at the time, I was thinking too slowly to question why he had sent them. It's interesting my lawyers didn't ask me, but then, you don't ask loonies about their lunacy. I imagine they were too embarrassed to mention it to me.

Anyway, two lawyers passed me around for eight years. Only the barrister was reasonable. When the lawyers did nothing, I would go and see him. He would tell them to do something, they would write one letter, and nothing for another year, until I demanded to see them again.

I stopped legal action eventually. We were coming up to the time we might have to go to court, and as no one believed me I couldn't see any point. Also, I discovered Mr. ...... had left his expensive offices under a financial cloud, so there was no point in suing him anyway. I hired a private investigator to confirm he had no money. I then discovered that he was a financial charlatan; in this case, he avoided paying his rent by taking his landlords to the Race Relations Tribunal.

For about eight years after therapy ended, I was consumed with anger. My only thought, every waking moment, was to control myself so that I didn't go down to his office and do him some harm. I also found I couldn't read. Recently, I found Hegel still on my bookshelf with a bookmark in it, on the same page as when the bomb dropped. I never recovered my concentration to finish it. For years, if I looked at a sentence, my memory wouldn't encompass the length of that sentence. I could just about read The Sun, but certainly nothing more advanced than that. I could read a bit of psychology where it was relevant to me. I scoured the backs of psychology books looking up "amnesia" or "short term memory loss" and found almost nothing. I looked up stuff on "shell shock" because it seemed something like it. The Second World War soldiers seemed to have been treated with a contempt that was familiar to me.

I had other symptoms. I couldn't feel physical sensation, I felt like a pair of eyes floating through space. I went for days without realising I needed to open my bowels until I felt pain. If I had put my fingers in the fire, I don't think I wouldn't have known until I smelled burning. I still went over and over the events I still felt overwhelmingly angry but I couldn't do anything about it. I went to jobs and held them down when I had no idea of what I was doing. At one typing job, my main concern was to keep my eyes moving, so no one would see how glazed I looked.

Louisa Street

I couldn't stop going over and over the events, and to some extent, I still can't. I also suffered from something I termed "mind-flip" which I see as a symptom of brainwashing. I would remember some of the outrageous things he had said to me, for example, "The reason you want to know is that you have never sublimated your subconscious aggression". This statement seemed unreasonable. Then I would do a "mind-flip" and I would see the same comments totally from his point of view and there would be no way to evaluate the two viewpoints. This was probably the most painful thing I have ever experienced, worse than my anger, worse than him rejecting me.

The following parable might explain the intensity of "mind-flip". Can you imagine you are in the street one day and you see the police lining up small children by the side of the road and shooting them? What would your reaction be? The ultimate in fear and horror! You would want to intervene or run away or scream or protest. But suppose, just before you could do that you did a "mind-flip" and your opinions became totally that of the police who were doing the killing. From their point of view, what they were doing would seem perfectly reasonable and for you, this terrible killing would also seem perfectly reasonable, even though you knew it wasn't. Now you can't act because they might be right, but you can't do nothing either, and that really would be torture. That was the analogy I worked out at the time. I made it that dramatic because it was the only way to explain to myself the strength of the pain I felt.

What I am trying to say here, is no matter what he did or said to me, I would "flip" to his point of view. It didn't matter that at first I would see it in my normal frame of mind, and see his action as wrong; because of the strength of his influence on me, I always ended up from his point of view, believing what he was doing was reasonable.

So, I went around in pain for ten, fifteen years. I had worked out that my memory loss and my going over and over the events were something to do with shell-shock, but it was only later that I sat in 42nd Street library in New York, found they had lots of books on memory loss and there was something called Post Traumatic Stress Disorder (PTSD). At the time, there was almost nothing in the UK on this topic. There were two books in the British Museum Library but I gave up when I found they wanted to interview me to find out why I wanted to read them. Books on PTSD hit the bookshelves in the UK about two years later, then at last, I could understand what was happening to me. By then, I could also go on the Internet.

Broken Boundaries

I remember, I sat on the steps of the beautiful 42nd Street library almost in tears because there were so many books and I couldn't read them. Even now, the thing I would like to do most would be to read books with the ease I did before. I can only read for about half an hour before I feel tired and the information doesn't stick.

Later, it all came on the Internet and I discovered other therapy survivors and cult survivors, such as survivors of the Church of Scientology, I found they routinely suffered from the same symptoms I did. However, when I tried to get help, I still couldn't because PTSD was considered only something that resulted from physical threats, so bad therapy wasn't included. In fact, cult and therapy situations can threaten the survival of your core values, the survival of the person you really are. I do consider a lot of therapy to be similar to a cult in that they are comprised of a charismatic leader and a set of irrational beliefs. Charisma can be a very dangerous quality.

Shortly after therapy ended, I was really scared of losing control. I went to see a physiotherapist who was offering hypnosis/relaxation. It really helped me. The feeling of being held back went and I realised this was simply tension. I also found that by relaxing and going over and over stressful situations in my mind, I could "iron them out" and they no long bothered me. He gave me the strength to cope. However, I still couldn't concentrate and I still couldn't read. I still had no physical sensation.

Later, I self medicated on illegal drugs. I managed to read Dr. Wm. Sergeant who wrote on shell-shock and its treatment with drug abreaction. With no one else to help me, I DIY'd my own drug abreaction with amphetamines and sodium amytal to release emotion. Once, it really worked and I got through to my full range of emotions, but it was too painful and I couldn't hold it. However, by doing this I managed to get back some physical and emotional sensation and I could read enough to get me through a post-graduate teaching course. In fact, this self experimentation did me less harm than the two legal psychiatric interviews I had. It took me a year or two to get over those.

I got through my teaching course. I wrote philosophy essays by writing all my ideas out then cutting and pasting them together. I couldn't remember the whole essay from start to finish, but I could make sure each paragraph followed on from the next.

From then on, I just struggled through each day. I held down part-time teaching jobs when I had no idea what I had done the day before, and no

Louisa Street

idea what I was doing the next day. I worked and still work as a journalist even though it takes me ages to get a piece together to make sense.

My memory is still substandard compared to what it was. I know I tried to tell someone about my memory problems when I was thirty and she said, "Maybe it's age". Its only now that I have the speed to answer daft statements like that. I still can't read for more than about thirty minutes without feeling tired. I can't remember names or faces but I've become expert in covering that up. Other people my age have a rich tapestry of their past to call on. I just have a grey blur. I wrote several pieces on the experience of amnesia, which got published, but I wrote them to make sense of it for myself.

There is a sequel to all this. About seven or eight years ago, (still no sense of time) I felt I needed to resolve the transference on my own. Because Mr. ...... had revealed nothing about himself, he still seemed all-powerful. I decided to investigate him. I researched him in the same way anyone else would research their ancestors. I knew when he had got divorced and started by getting his divorce certificate. I found out he had three different surnames, and his brother was a GP. This at least, gave me an idea why he had given himself a fake doctorate - I correctly diagnosed "brother envy". Then, about five years ago, I typed his name directly into my search engine and found his relatives were advertising for him on a UK missing person's website. I emailed the lady who had advertised and she phoned me. We had a long chat. He had a past. 40 years ago, he had dumped his wife and baby daughter and went off with prostitute. He then got a conviction for living on immoral earnings. Interesting, that he had been missing for 40 years and his nearest and dearest had never tried to find him before. One of his sisters didn't want to find him because she said he would only be after her money. The lady I talked to told me she found out there was a background of sexual abuse in the family. Maybe he was an abused child and that explains it.

She also confirmed my diagnosis of "brother envy". He had given himself a fake doctorate because his brother had been allowed to go to medical school and he had been taken away from school to work in the family business. She said he had never gotten over this. His lifetime grievance was that he was never allowed to go to university to study medicine. Well, Mr. ......, I got a degree and you didn't!

Anyway, when I found this out, I finally got him out of my head as a parent figure. Interestingly, by then, I had written several articles and was running a support group for people who had been damaged in therapy. I thought my story was unique but when I told my friend from my group what I had found out, she replied with a matching story of her own.

I now believe there is a pattern with some abusive therapists who are charismatic, manipulative and even carry psychopathic tendencies. These people have no feedback loop to moderate their own behaviour. A person who self-elects to enter therapy as a client, is by definition self-critical. When that person's world goes wrong, she doesn't blame other people, she tries to change herself. This is a philosophical stance that at least is open to question. In my theory, Anxiety Disorder (client) and Narcissistic Personality Disorder (therapist) latch onto each other in a horrible symbiosis.

Anyway, that was my experience. My therapist was a narcissist who revelled in the praise and adoration he got from his clients, but he couldn't stand criticism. All this therapy stuff about getting me to express my aggression was rubbish. When it came to it, he couldn't deal with my anger at all.

I still suffer to some extent from PTSD. My concentration and memory are still impaired. I can remember my very distant childhood. I can remember I had a polyphoto taken when I was aged 18 months, and they threw a teddy bear for me to catch, but the past thirty years are a grey blur.

Writing this down for WITNESS has helped. It's like I can now leave it with them and I can think about other things. My memory feels better. For the past few weeks, I have taken pride in remembering the date. I also went to a good hypnotherapist a few months ago and she stopped me obsessing about the events, although I still think about them quite often. I am also into meditation, something called "grounding meditation" and it helps a lot.

I just want to say, I never sat around and did nothing. I passed my degree. Afterwards, still suffering from amnesia, I studied with the Open University and passed Foundation Maths. I found Maths was easier to remember than English or Sociology because in Maths, the learning is sequential. One process helps you remember the next one. In English or Sociology, my degree subject, I couldn't remember the information and still find it hard to take in words and ideas.

Louisa Street

Because writing things down helped me, I intend to set up a notice board to help other survivors. I want my experience to help other people because if anything, I have to justify my life wasted by this experience. One last thing, in spite of what happened to me, I am proud of the fact that I, at least, took legal action against him.

4

Judith Field

The person I paid a lot of money to understand and accept me let me down to a more than anybody else in my life. She completely betrayed my trust. I went into therapy due to low self-esteem and lack of confidence, plus a lack of trust in others, which made it hard for me to make friends with people. I came out of therapy with an even greater lack of trust and a warped self-sufficiency that manifests in not even wanting to make friends.

I don't know if I can trust my readers to make up their own minds. I must first set the scene by explaining to you about events in my childhood; where my difficulties came from in the first place.

Here goes - when I first started school I had very poor speech. This was picked up upon by a group of boys two years older than me. Led by the Head's son they bullied me under the guise of helping me to talk. At the start of each playtime, before the duty teacher came out, they would frog march me to a hidden corner of the playground. There they would get me to say words I found difficult, either by asking me questions, or by getting me to repeat the words after them. For instance I couldn't say my Christian name and I couldn't say ambulance. They would start with easy words, such as things around us like gate, and then move onto the words I couldn't say. If I said a word and got it wrong they laughed, if I refused to try the word they would punch me in the stomach and wind me, kick me in the shins or bend my arm up behind me. In time I learned tactics to try and avoid them but it never crossed my mind to tell anybody. I just assumed that with their leader being the Head's son, that they could do what they liked. It must have gone on for months.

For the rest of my time at primary school I didn't make friends in my age group and there were episodes of teasing. I was always excluded by the other children and always the last to be picked for teams.

At secondary school I thought things were getting off to a better start when I apparently made a friend the very first week. The next week her primary school friend came back off holiday and took exception to me. I had told my new friend about starting my periods and all sorts of important things like that. When we were in sets for some subjects and her old friend wasn't around we got on fine together, like the first week, but when they were together they ignored me. Then things got worse. They involved other children off their school bus and they all started off by pestering me to answer their questions about what periods were like. I was too embarrassed to tell them what they wanted to know and so they resorted to trying to remove my under wear to find out if I was having a period at the time. Sooner or later they tired of this and would start playing a game of hide and seek in which I was also involved- or so I believed. Then when it was my turn to count and seek or else while I was hiding, they would all go off and leave me alone in the park.

The next major event in my life was losing my Dad very suddenly when I was 14. It was early in the school year and very few of my teachers knew me by name. I believed my bad behaviour had contributed to, or even caused my Dad's death - although it was really pretty normal teenage behaviour. I badly needed someone to confide in, someone who could reassure me, but I had to settle for day dreaming about talking to a particular teacher and it was my dreams that kept me going. I used to imagine this teacher putting her arm round me when I talked to her.

Outwardly I presented myself normally enough even though inside I felt desperate for some help. I just had to keep going and it was over twenty years before things finally caught up with me. By then I was at least happily married and we had two daughters. There were difficulties and I started confiding in another woman, who lived many miles away, by phone and letter. This sort of snow-balled and I belatedly realised I had become too dependant upon her and that this was totally inappropriate. I thought about being hugged by her and this really worried me. It seemed like I was resuming the daydreams I had had as a teenager.

Twelve years ago last Christmas, I faced up to the fact that I needed help and in the New Year I set about trying to get it. Twelve months on I wasn't much further forward. My GP had referred me to a Community Psychiatric Nurse (CPN) who offered me counselling for twelve to eighteen months, but then withdrew it after the first session because she was leaving. That summer I had had a handful of sessions from Relate (which were good) but not enough. My counsellor at Relate was great. At one session she quite spontaneously gave me a hug. That autumn I tried some group therapy as a result of being referred on by the CPN, but that didn't work for me because my need to talk was too great to cope with a group situation.

I spent almost the whole of the following year seeing a therapist in private practise, once a week, having resigned myself to the necessity to pay for help. During one of our first sessions I asked her if she ever hugged clients and she replied, "You only have to ask". I had a hug the next session but the following week she said she couldn't offer me any further hugs for the time being. For the rest of the time I was seeing her I kept trying to get her to change her mind again and then I decided to seek a therapist who would hug me because it seemed so important to me to be hugged. I had only made limited progress with her, perhaps because I was so obsessed with wanting to be hugged.

I drafted a letter that I sent out to eleven supervisors of counsellors/ therapists asking them if they knew of any practitioners who did hug clients. They all replied 'no' except Anna. She rang me to tell me that she did hug clients and she was able to take me on and would hug me. This seemed too good to be true - she was agreeing to hug me before we had even met. In that respect she was true to her word. I wound up my sessions with the other therapist and arranged to meet Anna as soon as I could.

I began seeing her in February 1997 and I had my first hug from her at my second session and from then on a hugs became an integral part of every session with Anna. For nearly two years I saw her almost every week and I made a lot of progress in many ways. Anna did some good work with me during that time. For example she did what she called regression therapy in which she pretended she had been there as a school counsellor at the time after my Dad died. We pretended that I had been able to confide in her then and after the session, she hugged and reassured me.

I regained the confidence to drive (which I hadn't done for several years) and she helped me gain confidence and self-esteem in other areas as well. She also helped me with social skills and I learnt to talk naturally to others for the first time in my life. She found it perfectly acceptable when I developed the same kind of obsession for her as I had done for the teacher at school. I became really dependant upon Anna and really attached to her and it felt as if I was in love with her. She not only accepted all that - she actively encouraged it. With hindsight, I can see that she basked in my admiration.

Quite apart from the hugging, another thing, which was always going to make the ending of my therapy harder for me, was that, she did not stick to any of the usual boundaries used by therapists. If she wasn't expecting another client after me she let me stay extra minutes. Sometimes I saw other clients coming or going. I didn't like to think about Anna seeing other clients but sometimes she would reassure me that I was special and if I told her I loved her she would sometimes tell me she loved me too. I quickly got into the habit of writing letters to Anna between sessions; even during the time I was still seeing her weekly. When I went on holiday Anna made me a tape recording of herself to take with me. I even rang her while I was away for about three years. Occasionally she gave me little presents and she told me that she didn't usually do that with clients.

Perhaps the highlight of my knowing Anna and the most significant of her boundary violations was three occasions when my two daughters and I went out with her and two similarly aged girls, who were the daughters of a former client who had died. On each occasion we went out in Anna's car and went for a walk somewhere and then went for a coffee together. This made me feel even more special because she obviously wasn't doing this with all her clients. After the third occasion Anna brought me back down to earth with a nasty bump by criticising how I was with my daughters. She also made it clear that this was the end of our outings together.

Anna told me a lot about herself and seemed to be prepared to answer any questions. I asked about her life or her past. Sometimes this went too far for my liking- because she would use my time to talk about herself. This probably balanced out with the times I stayed late. I was also able to ring Anna between sessions if I needed to and I think I did so rather more than necessary – before Anna became stricter about this later on. Of course, I didn't object to any of this. I knew that these sorts of things didn't usually happen with a therapist, but I believed that she was highly experienced (because she told me so) and that she knew what she was doing and how to handle things.

As I improved, I began to worry about whether I could continue to justify the expense of seeing her. When I discussed this with her, she said that it was too early to worry about that and by the time I was ready to finish therapy I would have made some friends. By then I wouldn't worry about not being able to see her any more and anyway, I could always stay in touch. I believed her and I did receive a lot of very good help and support from her which made it all the much harder for me when this all went so badly wrong.

Towards the end of my second year of seeing Anna she told me she was setting up a monthly all-day therapy group and she thought I needed to join the group if I was to progress further. I have to say I wasn't keen, but as Anna thought this was right for me I agreed to try it. It was all right the first time I attended the group and just about all right the second time. My notes show that from then onwards I found it a difficult experience. (I have always kept notes on both my individual and my group therapy sessions). After that things went steadily down hill, not just at the group days but there was also an effect on my individual sessions with Anna.

Soon after the second group day, I had a very bad individual session with Anna. She got really angry with me and twice she walked out of the room and left me. This was because I was talking about why I hadn't got friends and Anna said I knew why this was and she wanted me to tell her, but I couldn't give the answer she was looking for and this made her angry. That night I couldn't sleep very well because I kept going over what had happened with Anna.

There were between four and eight women in Anna's group each time, the way it worked was that one person at a time would be talking to Anna while the other people listened. Anybody could offer a comment or question to the person if they wanted to. Sometimes either a client or Anna would suggest doing a psychodrama or another exercise instead of just talking. Each person might have anything from 15 minutes to two hours depending upon Anna's discretion. This meant that not everybody would necessarily have a turn. It was a matter of speaking up at the right time - and knowing when that was. This was one of my difficulties with being there. Sometimes I would sit patiently waiting all day and then not get a turn because I hadn't asked. Other times I would try to get in when

Broken Boundaries

I thought the person had finished and then be told that they hadn't. When somebody did finish it seemed as if other people were always quicker to jump in than me.

Most of the group were trainee therapists themselves and so were more advanced with their own development and this seemed to be much of the problem for me. Nobody made any allowances for me, especially Anna herself - no doubt everybody else took their cue from her any way. It seemed to me as if she forgot who I was at the group and left me behind because of having so many people to think about. All the others were capable of looking after themselves in these circumstances but this was my difficulty to begin with. I really tried my hardest at the group month after month but every time I would come home upset and irritable with my long-suffering family.

At the third group day I had my first experience of being unable to follow and keep up with what was happening. I found it emotionally draining and was left feeling overwhelmed when I lost track of what was going on. Sometimes I felt jealous of the other group members seemingly grabbing Anna's full attention. On the other hand, often when I did get to say things at the group I often wished I hadn't because once I got in the limelight I found it difficult to get out of it again.

During my third year with Anna I continued seeing her individually once a week between the group days. At this stage most of these individual sessions continued to seem helpful on the whole. Around this point I still believed what Anna told me - that I needed to attend the group to improve further.

My admiration for Anna was such that I wanted to follow in her footsteps and to give something back, so I did two preliminary counselling courses at this time. Part of the reason I started training as a counsellor was because of my own long search for help and then thinking it had been worth the wait when I met Anna; I wanted to make it easier for other people to get help.

However by the autumn of that year I was having a rough time at the group each month but Anna kept insisting she knew what she was doing and it was all in my own interest. Sometimes others in the group would cautiously question what she was doing with me but she reassured them that she was highly experienced and knew how to handle my type of difficulty.

Judith Field

After my seventh time at the group I wrote in my notes for the first time about feeling that Anna was bullying me at the group. I wrote that I told the group I hadn't got anything in particular I wished to do but there were one or two unconnected things I wished to share with them. I explained about being away for two of the last four weeks since we had last met and not talking to anybody else during that time apart from meeting up with a lady who I supported as a befriender. Someone asked why I was telling them this. I replied that I was reporting where I was up to, which is what I had heard the others doing. I said that I had hoped to go to my Mum's the next weekend but might not be able to, explaining why and why we couldn't stay with my siblings.

Then, from the group's reactions, I felt I was being put on the spot. Somehow we had got into the situation of Anna waiting for me to say something and me crying because I felt I had been backed into a corner and I felt threatened and got at. We broke for lunch without solving anything.

As soon as we began again after lunch Anna asked me if I had had any thoughts over lunch. I said that as soon as it had been my turn I had felt as if I was being threatened, put on the spot and got at and yet when it was someone else's turn it didn't seem to me that they were being got at. Anna seemed pleased with my coherent reply and asked if I felt got at that moment, and I said 'no'. I was asked why and I said I thought it was because I felt refreshed after the break. Anna said she didn't think it was that but I forgot what she said. But then Anna quickly seemed to drive me into a corner again. I lost complete track of everything just after that. I was crying and felt really hot and uncomfortable about feeling I had been put on the spot again and I got really upset. I did not know what was expected from me. At one point I tried to leave the room because of feeling so hot and bothered, but Anna said the contract I had signed said I couldn't do that. Anna said I could open the window but I said I didn't know if other people would mind.

I thought everybody was waiting for a response from me but I did not know what response they wanted. I sat there feeling worse and worse, I thought an answer was expected from me but I said I didn't know there had been a question. Anna kept asking me to look at her and the others and then she wanted me to ask them if they were laughing at me. I asked Janet and then I said it was too hard and I felt dizzy. At that point Anna invited me over to sit by her and I gradually recovered as Georgina and then Janet had their turn.

Broken Boundaries

When it was the summing up bit at the end I was last to speak and I said I felt totally confused. Anna made me ask each of the group in turn, by name, if they accepted me and if they wanted me in the group because she said she was afraid of what I might make of it all later. This baffled me a bit because it was her who had been getting at me.

In the evening I rang Helen (from the group). I told Anna about falling out with my husband because I had come home in a mood again.

Two days later I was still feeling really upset about what had happened and I managed to speak to Anna on the phone about it. I told her about believing she had set up the situation at the group so that I would feel the same as I did when I was bullied at school. I thought this was part of a plan so that I would learn to deal with it better. Anna appeared shocked at this suggestion and said she would never do that to me because that wasn't the way she worked. At my next individual session Anna explained that it was because I had been bullied at school that I saw bullying taking place when it wasn't and she said my perception of things was wrong. I felt reassured by what she said but it didn't last. Nevertheless, for a time, things did improve a little.

When I looked back at my notes I could almost see a pattern of things being worse at the individual sessions which immediately followed the group days and then things picking up again at my one to one sessions just before the next group day. At least that was the case while I continued to see Anna each week between the group days.

During my one-to-one sessions she wouldn't discuss the group with me, except to say that I needed to carry on with it for it to work. Sometimes I asked Anna whether she thought I was ready to reduce my sessions but each time I raised this Anna said I had a long way to go yet and it wasn't time to consider this. Early into the second year of the group, I began reducing my individual sessions with Anna. We agreed on one individual session per month to fall mid-way between the group days. I carried on like this throughout 2000. This was partly because my job was coming to an end around the middle of the year and my attempts to find a new job were not going well. I knew I wouldn't be able to afford therapy if I wasn't working and also because Anna had raised the price of my individual sessions. She lessened the cost of group days for me because she said she thought it was more worthwhile for me to attend the group days.

Once I was seeing her less often one-to-one, it seemed as if she was losing touch with me generally. Anna sometimes said things like I still hadn't learnt to trust her and that I hadn't made a therapeutic alliance with her. This puzzled me because of the depth of our relationship in the first two years.

After that things were sort of up and down for me at the group. Sometimes I said as little as possible and didn't suggest any work I wanted to do while there; but this left me feeling I had wasted my money by going at all that month. At other times, when I did go there with an idea of what I wanted to do, I might not get the opportunity to do anything; and I would come away feeling really let down and frustrated. Then there were also times when Anna said I was planning too much what I wanted to do instead of suggesting an idea and seeing how it developed. Whatever I said or did at the group, I never seemed to get things right and yet it seemed that other people were allowed to say and do things without all this trouble. Although I knew the bigger picture of why I was in therapy it was difficult for me to present something I could work on in the group.

I frequently said that I wanted to leave the group and I tried repeatedly to discuss this with Anna. Every time I did she reassured me that I was improving – although I could no longer see it. Anna said I had to expect it to be difficult if it was to be of benefit to me. She said I needed to stick with it and trust the process - that it would be worth it in the end. If I said I was just going to leave the group Anna said I wouldn't be able to continue seeing her individually either.

So I continued to attend every month even though I found it increasingly distressing. Perhaps Anna was right about me needing to be in a group, but I don't think that group under her leadership was right for me.

Of course, you may well ask why I didn't just leave the group if things were that bad. With hindsight I believe I should have left therapy with Anna after the first two years, instead of going on to join the group. But then hindsight is a wonderful thing. There was of course my attachment to Anna and my wish to continue seeing her as things had been so good before. Indeed there were still some times when the therapy was helpful, particularly during my individual sessions.

Even at the group things could be all right when I wasn't under the spot light. Lunch times at Anna's house with the group were lovely and it could be interesting seeing and watching what other people did when it was their turn to do therapy. This wasn't because I was sadistic because mostly other people did not get upset the way I did. There were times when others were upset but not with the frequency that I was.

Overall I was still feeling positive enough about my therapy to begin doing the certificate in counselling skills course.

It was at about this same time when I again mentioned in my notes about feeling that Anna was bullying me at the group. On this occasion I was put in the familiar position where Anna kept asking me questions I couldn't answer. The more I tried to think and the more she pressed me for an answer the more stressed I became and I got into a panic so that I couldn't think straight at all. The point from feeling all right to feeling got at seemed to happen suddenly. It led me to conclude that this was because when I was being bullied as a child, I didn't even know what was happening to me was wrong, and so I would have suddenly become upset then too.

I noted at this point that I asked Anna if she regretted taking me into the group, but she said no. It was a question I was to ask her again but each time she gave the same answer. It was still a full year before my worst day at the group.

At around this point I also had a different kind of bad experience in my one to one therapy with Anna. At this session Anna seemed really tired to the point of being sleepy. I asked her about it and she explained about having a very late night. I left feeling cheated and that evening, I had the worst argument with my then teenage daughter that I had ever had before or since. The next day I rang Anna as I wanted to tell her about what had happened. She said she didn't need to know but I said I needed to tell her. She said I wanted to tell somebody but it need not be her. I told her I felt cheated about her not being with me during the session. She said "I know" but she still wouldn't let me tell her about the argument.

As with the bad group sessions it took a while to (apparently) recover our relationship.

In the autumn, just over six years ago, I experienced a bad time at the group, which was also different to the other bad times, thus far. The difference was that it was actually Janet and not me who was doing therapy at the time.

Judith Field

That October Janet did some work around the subject of her brother being born when she was 19 months old. She was enacting the experience from her childhood of seeing her brother receiving the attention from their mum which she so desperately craved herself. Janet's work took place on the floor in the middle of the circle of chairs using cushions. To begin with Anna was aware that this work might resonate with me and invited me to kneel down on the floor on her left side, while she attended to Janet on her right, so that I could make contact with her if I wanted to.

At the start Janet was talking about what had happened and that her brother seemed to get all the love and attention. I listened with great interest and secretly I felt sceptical about whether she could actually remember what happened when she was that young. Nevertheless it did seem as if she was giving words to what I believed had probably happened to me too. Then she began to cry and wail loudly and Anna gradually moved round to face her to try and support and help her. All Anna's attention was now on Janet as she cried out loudly in her distress. I couldn't move with Anna very well because of the positions of the chairs behind us and it would have seemed intrusive to have stood up and moved around.

As the situation became more and more uncomfortable and then painful for me, I fiddled with the tassels/fringe on a throw and a floor cushion. I was aware of other group members leaving the room– probably to go to the toilet, and it seemed as if I was alone in the room with Janet and Anna. Although I never was, it seemed that way to me, partly because of kneeling on the floor so that I couldn't see any body else very well. I was aware of a sense of panic and being scared that I had been abandoned.

Then everything became more and more distant as if I were observing it from a long way off, it was as if I were going to faint. Everything was really remote and far away and I didn't think I could move or speak. Suddenly I became aware of Anna calling me back and talking sharply to me and telling me off. She said I was acting out and spoiling Janet's piece of work by attempting to join in when this hadn't been contracted. Then I couldn't stop myself sobbing and so one of the others - a trainee therapist was asked to take me out of the room until I could be quiet.

When I came back Anna told me off for disrupting Janet's work, which left me feeling really let down. I was upset and bewildered by this because I had done all I could to let the work continue without interrupting. Anna claimed she had offered me her arm and I had ignored it. I wasn't aware of this at all. If she did offer her arm it was too late to reach me. Even after that Anna still seemed cross with me. I felt disturbed for several days afterward by what had happened to me. I was sure I couldn't help what had happened and yet Anna seemed to think I could.

Much worse was to come. Compared to what was to happen six months later what had already happened was nothing. The worst day for me, the one which led to me making a complaint which ultimately ended Anna's career, took place six months later. By then I had been seeing Anna for more than four years altogether and the group had been running for over two years.

At the group in March 2001 Anna made a big issue about me not trusting her enough for my therapy to be successful. I was still deeply attached to her because she could still be really nice to me; and I desperately wanted to show her that I did trust her and so I tried to take this on board. However, the therapy would break down beyond repair in the following month.

When we began that April, I could see some of the letters I had written to Anna on the floor. Anna asked if I wanted to read them out to the group or if I wanted her or someone else to read them out. I said I would read out bits myself as I could read out the meaning as I intended. I began reading from the first page of the first letter and never got any further because Anna challenged me on everything I read out.

Then Anna said she had been talking to an American therapist friend, about me. She had suggested that my problems stem from before birth and something to do with perhaps not being fully accepted during pregnancy and perhaps not wanted. In response to this Fiona suggested a piece of work in which I was to be tied to a radiator. Anna asked if I wanted to do a piece of work like this or to carry on with the letters. I was left to think about it during the morning lunch break. Susan, another group member, said that if there was a piece of work about being tied up then to count her out because idea of being tied to someone was so awful to her, she would kill the other person.

I can't remember all the details of what happened after break but I did say I would do the piece of work. It was suggested that I was tied up to a bad mother figure and I had to break loose at some point and reach out to Anna. Then I would be tied to her and go round attached to her by a scarf and then take home the scarf that had been round Anna. I was asked which scarf I would want to take home. Anna asked for a volunteer to be the bad mother. Susan volunteered. This moved Anna and two others to tears because of her volunteering in spite of what she had said earlier. Anna produced a third scarf and then some belts. It was decided the bad mother would be fixed to me with the more harsh belts and then I would be tied to Anna by softer scarves.

I was asked if I remembered anything relevant about my pre - birth. I said that my parents lived in a caravan for the first three years of their marriage until I came along. But it was taken that they still lived in the caravan after my birth, that my parents were young and that my Mum had misgivings, at the very least about having me. None of this fits with what I know from my Mum. We began the role-play with me attached to Susan with the belts and us standing on a large mat to represent the caravan. Susan thrashed around as if trying to shake me off and get rid of me but I just went with her and was passive because the scenario didn't fit for me at all. It was then decided that the idea wasn't working in this format because of my passivity. I was asked how I felt but I didn't note my actual response.

Things suddenly moved fast, but I wasn't in on what was being talked about or decided upon. Anna said she thought I needed a rebirthing process and she went out of the room and came back with a sheet and I was asked to sit on a chair close up to a mirror. The sheet was placed over me making a tent. Anna told me I was to be left like this and I had to ask the universe when I wanted to come out when I'd had enough. This was supposed to represent my birth. I reluctantly agreed to this piece of work despite my reservations.

I was left under the sheet whilst everyone went to lunch. At 2.40pm everybody came back, by which time I had been there about 1¼ hours. I asked if I could come out but Anna said I wasn't asking as if I meant it and so I had to stay there. Then I was asked if I wanted to come out and I said yes. Anna set up another mirror to my left and there followed a short scenario. I was asked if I wanted to go back to the Mum in the caravan or another Mum. I said I needed to know more - because I didn't know what I was supposed to say. I was asked if I would go to a substitute Mum called Anna who was a therapist. I said yes. I was asked what I wanted from her but I said I didn't know. I was asked to think about it and to let them know when I had. It was nearly 3pm then.

Now I didn't know what to do. I had thought that I only had to ask and to mean it, to be allowed out. It seemed as if the goal posts had definitely been moved and I thought that I had been tricked into doing this work.

Broken Boundaries

At that point someone else started talking about their stuff and so I didn't want to interrupt to ask what I had to do and so I just sat and cried quietly to myself. I no longer knew what was expected of me and I thought everybody had plotted a new agenda while they were down at lunch. Sometimes I was too lost and upset even to bother crying and sometimes I did listen to what else was being said, but I couldn't hear well enough all the time. They mostly ignored me and carried on talking about other peoples' issues. I partly listened in to work by three others.

Often I thought that perhaps I was experiencing what it would be like to be dead, able to hear some of what was going on in a remote kind of way, but not be able to take any part of it.

I wasn't sure if I should ask questions or whether that would show I didn't trust enough. Sometimes I asked what I had to do to be allowed out and sometimes Anna allowed Fiona to ask me questions about what I had to do to be allowed out. To me this came across as if she was goading me. This increased as the afternoon went on. I cried quietly on and off the whole time.

Eventually while Susan was doing her work there was a pause and I took the opportunity to speak up. I forget the exact sequence of what was said. I said I wanted to get out from being under the sheet. I was asked if I knew what I had to do. I said I thought I had done what had been asked of me and I said I had had enough of the game. I was asked if I would answer the question I had been left with. I said yes I did want to go to the therapist called Anna but I couldn't say what I wanted from her other than to learn to connect with people. Fiona said yes this was OK but I was not allowed to stop at this. I was asked what else I wanted. I said to get out from under the sheet.

We seemed to go round in circles with Fiona saying I wasn't asking properly. Anna kept giving a count down of how much time was left. This made me feel even more anxious because I was afraid that after all the time I had been under the sheet that the work might be declared a failure and I might be told I hadn't done it right. I asked what else did I have to say but still they said I wasn't being clear about what I wanted. I was asked if I wanted to give up the piece of work several times or whether I wanted to see it through. I said I had to see it through because I didn't want everything left up in the air and I didn't want to have been through all that for nothing.

Again we seemed to go round in circles. It might have been about them wanting me to put more energy into it. I became anxious about the prospect of them calling off the piece of work as I had gone along with it for so long when I was desperate to get out. I said it was getting claustrophobic being under the sheet so long. I asked about the bit about being tied to Anna with the scarf but they said the plans had been changed from this and acted as though they expected me to realise this. I was asked why I didn't just move the sheet myself but I said I didn't know I was allowed to do this and I thought I had to keep to the rules. I suggested that Anna removed the sheet from me as she had put it there. Fiona kept asking me what I wanted when I came out and what I would be satisfied with and I said a hug from Anna.

When I was finally allowed out after more than 4½ hours under the sheet everybody clapped. I was shaking and parched and I felt weak at the knees. Anna asked me if I wanted some food or to be held first but my mouth was really dry, so I said neither and asked for a drink of water first. Janet got me a glass of water and I had over a glass full. As soon as I thought about food I felt really nauseous. Anna held me while Susan finished her work and the group began summing up. Soon we went downstairs but I continued to feel weak at the knees and I felt really disorientated.

The sight of food in the kitchen made me feel even more nauseous. Anna kept offering me food but I refused it. She gave me a bag of food to take home and I continued to refuse the rest of what she offered. My mouth still felt really dry. Jackie did some exercises with me to help me get grounded enough to drive home - looking and listening carefully to what was in the room. I sat on a chair in the kitchen for several minutes. I felt aware of some things and yet strangely detached in other ways. It must have been nearly 7pm by the time I left. Anna didn't seem to pay much attention to me other than offering me the food.

I wrote other notes on the day about being left under the sheet: 'like a shroud, group colluding against me, like being dead, gave up quickly when left alone, made fun of? Thought it was about trusting, - paradox - trust or strike out.' It felt like things were done to me, out of my control, I felt like a pawn rather than a victim. I felt resentful about being left under the sheet so long and missing dinner break. I had hoped to show some photographs I had taken previously at Anna's and I had hoped to take some more.

Broken Boundaries

That evening I rang Anna six times because of my continuing distress about what had happened and that night I had the first of several bad dreams about it. I dreamed that a man was in our house trying to attack me with a machete but I was covered with a sheet and so I couldn't see where the blows were coming from to avoid them and I was getting more tangled up in the sheet the more I tried to remove it. I rang Anna's number and left a message on her answer phone at 4.30am in the morning saying how upset I felt. In the morning I rang and spoke to her.

I was desperate to talk to Anna and to try and understand why she had put me through this and for her to know how I felt about it, but when I saw her individually, which was once later in April and once in May, she said it was group work and could only be discussed at the group. At that point she refused to give me another appointment to see her individually and therefore my last individual session with Anna was in May that year.

It seemed a really long wait until the group met five weeks later in May, but when the day finally came I couldn't get space to talk about it and Anna seemed to be blocking me from talking. She completely failed to understand why I felt upset and I began to question all the understanding she had apparently previously shown me.

At the group day, I said that I felt as if I was still under the sheet from last time, as if I was seeing everything from a detached, unconnected place and things weren't getting through to me. I said that I felt that I had given up and that I felt aloof from things; as if everything was going on over my head and that I was in limbo. I explained that I had had a really difficult five weeks since the last time there and that I had had all sorts of problems. I said it felt like everything was too much effort and that I felt like I was still under the sheet. I had given up and was on auto pilot, affected by things directly relating to me but in a selfish way as if other people's stuff didn't touch me. At some point someone said I wasn't making a lot of sense. Fiona, Janet and Anna were all saying things to me and I felt as if I was in a corner with everyone attacking me. Fiona said that I was in a good place if I was detached from other people. When we got downstairs I asked Anna for a hug, which she gave me and she said she was sorry I was in such an uncomfortable place. I started to cry.

The next time we met up, I was late. When I got to Anna's it was 10.15am and Susan arrived at the same time. I was going to use the toilet and get a drink before I went in the room but I wanted to go in at the same time as Susan to cut down on interruptions – and because I didn't want to go in alone. I got a cup of tea and then realised Susan was going in the room ahead of me and so I quickly followed her taking my drink with me. There wasn't a seat for me in the circle as there were already eight group members there with Anna, so I sat at the back thinking I would finish my tea and then move my chair at a suitable point. Straight away Anna told me off for sitting there. She said, "You're not staying there" in a hostile manner. Jackie beckoned me to sit on a cushion between her and the radiator. I went over but the heat from the radiator was such that I knew I couldn't stay there so I went and knelt down in a gap between Rachel and June but again, Anna said I wasn't to stay there.

She then realised I had a cup of tea and told me off for bringing it into the room and she told me I knew the rules. I said I had seen others in the room with such drinks and Anna said other people always asked permission first and I said that I didn't know they had. She sent me out of the room to finish my drink.

I sat on the top step of the stairs and drank my tea in great gulps because I had a lump in my throat and I cried a bit. When I headed back to the room I thought I felt OK but when I got there I cried a bit more. June made room for me to sit on the end of the sofa beside her but I didn't have enough room and I wasn't comfortable. Therefore I sat on the floor and leaned against the wall. After break I got some cushions and sat in the same place. It was OK there really. Later I was able to sit on the sofa, because Susan and Fiona had left early.

When I arrived it had been Tina who was talking. At break, Anna gave me a hug and I explained why I was late. After break, Susan talked briefly about leaving and as there were so many of us, Anna said she wanted us all to say something between then and 1pm. I kept attempting to get in but each time somebody beat me to it. Eventually I managed to get twenty-seven minutes.

As soon as I spoke, Anna asked me why I was smiling. I said it was a relief at being able to get to speak as I had been trying so hard. Anna said it didn't look like that to her, it looked like gallows laughter. Anna said to me that I didn't ever hear the positive things which people say to me and also that I don't answer when somebody asks me a question. This is because I often think that they are trying to trip me up and get at me. Anna also accused me of playing a game around what ever it was I was doing.

It was at this point that we stopped for lunch. Only Julie had yet to speak. Susan and Fiona said they would leave at the end of the lunch break.

Broken Boundaries

When we began again after lunch break, I stated that I wanted to ask a question about the sheet work. I asked whether I needed to stay under the sheet that long or if I could have just come out. Anna said that the decision was mine and it was entirely up to me whether I had stayed there or come out and I didn't need anybody's permission. At that point Janet reminded me that Julie had yet to speak and said I couldn't do any work yet. After Julie had spoken Tina did some cushion work and this was talked about and then Jackie did some work. When Jackie finished I was allowed ten minutes before closing statements and signing off began.

I said I wanted to check out some things related to the sheet work. I said I had had no idea that I could have come out until somebody from the group had told me that over the phone. I said that I thought I had to trust what was happening and had I entirely missed the point and I stayed there all that time for nothing? I asked, "So you believe that I chose to stay there all that time?" and "So from your frame of reference I could have come out?" Anna told me that the point was I needed to be myself and do what I had to do. She said I didn't have to abide by any rules because there weren't any. It was about trusting, about trusting the process and doing what I had to do. Anna said that I hadn't stayed there for nothing. She said it had been useful.

Julie said I reminded her of the song "There's a hole in my bucket" because she said I just seemed to go round in circles, asking for help but not getting anywhere. She said that was because I wasn't stating what I wanted. When I was asked for my closing statement last of all I said I was confused and frustrated. Anna said something about accepting that I was confused for the time being. Janet made a statement about my lack of progress. I started crying again and said something about people saying I kept going over the same ground and so I was not given the opportunity to actually do any work. Anna asked me who had said that. I said that Janet had. Janet then explained it again in more detail and I realised that she was suggesting that what was being done to me wasn't working and perhaps something different should be tried. But Anna said it was working because I was progressing in some ways. (In spite of the group?)

As Anna had seemed to be really angry with me about everything I tried to do or say all day and I couldn't really get space to talk about the sheet work I became even more convinced Anna was blocking me from talking about it.

After that I rang Anna's therapy organisation but they said they could only address my concerns if I put them in writing and so I sent in a letter worded as a complaint.

When I attended the group in July I told Anna about my complaint and she seemed very shocked and said it could harm her career. At that point I didn't want to do that and so I withdrew the complaint although it hadn't been regarded as an official complaint anyway because I hadn't been through enough channels first.

Anna did let me talk about what had happened to a limited extent both at the July and August group days, although she would not give me adequate answers about why she had left me under the sheet so long. She still wouldn't really talk about it with me and she was still showing no understanding of why it had upset me so much. It was only at that point that she told me that the purpose of the sheet work had been to get me out of trying to please her all the time and the idea had been for me to get fed up with being left under the sheet and to come out without permission and that the expectation had been that I would get out and just go down and have lunch with everybody.

I can understand why I wasn't told this before the sheet work but surely Anna should have known me well enough to know that this idea was never going to work with me. Also only a month earlier she had made that big issue about me not trusting her and so I thought I needed to do as I was told and stay there until she gave me permission to come out. My need to please her was too strong and surely my reasons for this were obvious. The irony was that I had wanted to be hugged to know that I was acceptable and yet the affect of being left alone under the sheet and Anna's apparent abandonment of me seemed to undo any growing sense of acceptance I had had.

I was still far from happy about the situation. When I attended the group in September I tried to talk about something different to see if it was possible to just try and carry on. This wasn't very satisfactory for me because I had lost the chance to see Anna individually and I wanted to try and get her full support back.

After September 11th I quickly began seeing a person-centred counsellor because I realised I still needed some ongoing individual support and also help in getting over what had happened with Anna. I was seeing Pat regularly for twenty-two months and throughout this time most of what I talked about with her was about what went wrong with Anna and my loss of her support and understanding. Pat was very good at understanding my thoughts and feelings. I couldn't fault her at all. Pat's boundaries were very strict and so I felt safe with her and I trusted her which I thought was pretty positive after what I have been through. Pat described herself as a counsellor rather than a therapist and charged less that therapists do. I think she was used to doing relatively short-term work with clients.

I got really angry with Anna when I attended her group in October.

Early in November I spoke to Anna on the phone three times and it began to seem that she was trying to sort things out between us. I also thought I might be making some head-way with getting her to understand about how the sheet work had been for me. The following week Anna rang me to say that she had breast cancer and that she was about to have a mastectomy – to be followed by six months of chemotherapy and so the group was being suspended indefinitely. I hadn't told Pat that I had still been attending the group but at that point I had to. When she found out she said that she thought the group was so harmful to me that she was not prepared to continue seeing me unless I resigned from the group. She said she could see the distress it was continuing to cause me.

It could have been a tough choice but to me at that stage the answer was obvious – I had to resign from the group. I didn't want to go back to the group because I found it so difficult there and it didn't seem to be getting me anywhere. Nobody knew how long it would be before the group could continue anyway. I sent a handwritten note to all the group members letting them know of my decision not to return to the group. Three of the eight people in the group acknowledged this with lovely notes wishing me well and so forth. I thought I ought to wait until Anna was a bit better before I told her. I stayed in regular phone contact with Jackie for a while and she was supportive and did not blame me for what happened at the group, although at the same time she remained loyal to Anna. Susan had been so upset by the sheet work that she left the group in June. The week before Christmas 2001, I paid a brief social visit to Anna. I rang her once each the two following weeks to see how she was. Then the next week when I rang her, she put the phone down on me and cut me off. After that I thought I would do my best to get by without her. I still didn't inform her of my decision to leave the group because I thought I didn't want to trouble her with therapy issues if it wasn't even acceptable to ring to see how she was while she was still so poorly.

Then in February 2002 Anna left me a phone message saying I could phone her on Monday if I liked because she was feeling a bit better.

However when I got home from work that Monday I found an angry phone message from her saying that I should have informed her of my decision to leave the group and that I had broken my contract. She had spoken to someone in the group about running the group the following Monday, as a one off, and they had told her that I was leaving the group. I rang her again to speak to her about it and again she hung up on me. I then sent her a letter about leaving the group in time for her to share if with the group if she wanted to.

I still had lots of unanswered questions I wanted to put to her, and so, thinking she could not be feeling too bad if she was able to run the group, I wrote to her again with sixty three questions I wanted to ask. She then offered me a one-off session as closure so long as I brought somebody else with me because she did not want to see me alone. I took along a friend who was a trainee counsellor and the meeting took place that March. The meeting was helpful to some extent even though Anna was still being very defensive and wasn't giving adequate answers and I didn't get the chance to ask many of my questions.

However, the meeting turned out to be unsatisfactory for me as so much was still left unresolved that I was still unable to move on. I contacted Anna's organisation again in May 2002 with a view to making a complaint and they gave me contact details of one of their members who could help me negotiate with her. He suggested I set up another meeting with Anna. We had another meeting in June with the same witness present as before. I still wasn't satisfied with what she said to me - especially as she was twisting the facts to suit herself on several crucial points – such as saying I knew I was to be left alone in the room under the sheet when I agreed to it. But I would never have agreed to it if I had known that, and anyway, how was I possibly going to ask to come out if there was no one there to ask? Anna said she had never called it "rebirthing" and I had made that up. She also claimed I showed no sign of being upset on the day or immediately afterwards - although I had rung her to report nightmares and difficulty sleeping etc. How could she know how upset I was when I was alone in the room under the sheet for over an hour and still hidden by the sheet after that for a total of over four hours?

Although both these sessions had been helpful up to a point Anna still refused to acknowledge that she had made any mistakes. She was still saying that I was making a fuss over nothing. In July 2002 I went ahead and made an official complaint to her organisation.

Broken Boundaries

They wrote back to me in September saying that their assessor said it required proper investigation. Then in November they wrote again asking, "In what way (I) would experience a sense of resolution which would enable me to move on with (my) life."

In my reply I asked for three things and first and foremost of these was an apology from Anna so long as she could genuinely give me this, preferably face-to-face.

I also asked for help in reaching an understanding of what was happening while I was attending Anna's group and how she could have missed it. The third thing I wanted to happen as a result of my complaint was that I wanted Anna to be required to have the recommended amount of supervision. A long time back when things had been OK she told me she was so experienced that she did not need supervision.

A month after their last letter to me Anna's organisation wrote to me again saying the complaint wasn't being upheld but they were arranging a meeting between Anna and me with a facilitator present. A date had already been set by them for middle of January 2003 at a place about sixty miles away from where both Anna and I lived.

I didn't really see the point of another meeting and so I wrote back saying so, but they said that was all that was on offer. I went through with it because I harboured a hope that Anna was going to apologise at the meeting.

The meeting turned out similar to the two previous meetings. It went OK, but as I expected it didn't really achieve much. It had been set for a maximum time of 1½ hours and the first hour was spent talking over various things - mostly raised by me. Anna and I still ended up disagreeing on the same points as before and amazingly Anna changed a couple of things from what she had previously said and when I challenged her she said she had said these things all along.

Anna still refused to even acknowledge that anything had gone wrong in my therapy. I could not understand why she could not admit that doing that work with me was a serious mistake and why she was unable to help me deal with it.

Each time Anna and I disagreed the facilitator just moved us on to another point and didn't cast any opinions himself. At the end of an hour he said we needed to think about closure and saying a final goodbye. This took the whole remaining half hour available but at least this meeting ended on a much better note than my previous meeting with Anna in June.

At the end I was annoyed to find out that Anna and the facilitator knew each other quite well and so the whole thing seemed like a white wash.

After the January meeting I told Anna's organisation I wished to appeal but they said it was too late and I should have done so instead of attending the meeting. This made me really angry and so in February 2003 I contacted the UKCP and asked if I could appeal through them. The UKCP agreed that I could appeal but nothing more happened for months.

I wrote to Anna several times following the meeting and then followed my letters up with a phone call each time. It was when I spoke to Anna in May that she realised that I had not seen her written response to my complaint and she told me that she had expected that I would see it. I contacted her organisation again and they sent me a copy of Anna's letter.

When I saw the letter, I wasn't surprised that they had not upheld the complaint. She had twisted everything that did not show her in a good light and made it look as if I was the one who had lied. I was shocked at how many things I disagreed with in her letter. There was so much Anna said that just wasn't true. This made me feel even angrier since she had clearly had a copy of what I had said; yet I hadn't got to see her response until her organisation thought the matter was closed.

I wrote back to her organisation enclosing a copy of Anna's letter with all the things highlighted which I disagreed with and included my response or version to those items.

Obviously it was my word against hers with nearly all of it. But why did she lie so much if she had expected me to see what she said? It is clear to me that she must have known that the truth would not look good for her. No doubt she was afraid about the outcome if the truth had come out. How glad she must have been when nobody challenged the things in her letter. I knew I couldn't actually prove most of the things I disagreed with; but I was just so angry that it hadn't even got as far as a hearing. Was Anna that confident that she would be believed instead of me? So where did all this leave me? I realised that it was no wonder that the investigator from her organisation reached a different conclusion to their assessor because the investigator was going by Anna's version of it all, which was wrong. I believe their assessor only saw what I had told them. What reason would I have to lie about it all? I was not after compensation after all - just an apology and an acknowledgement that what happened should not have happened.

Then in October 2003, exactly 2½ years after the sheet work, the UKCP wrote again saying I could make an appeal through them.

The UKCP set up an appeal hearing for the end of March 2004. Sukey[1], from POPAN (which is now called WITNESS), who had been supporting me over the phone, met me in London so that she could offer me support at the hearing. However it couldn't go ahead after all. As soon as it started the UKCP said they couldn't hold an appeal hearing as there hadn't been a hearing by Anna's organisation first. I couldn't believe I had waited a year without this being picked up. Then I learnt that because of having this aborted UKCP appeal hearing Anna's organisation were obliged to say that they would hold a hearing themselves after all. They first set this up for July 2004 but then postponed it until September. This turned out to be because Anna was refusing to cooperate.

The hearing finally took place in Birmingham in September 2004 and this time I was supported by John[2] from POPAN. Anna had her husband with her. I was really nervous about it but I conducted myself in a much better way than Anna did. Four of the five group members who had been there on the day of the sheet work had supplied written witness statements in support of Anna and agreed with her that I was aware that I was to be left alone in the room under the sheet. When I had seen their statements shortly before the hearing I thought I didn't stand a chance. However I argued that their statements were so similarly wrong that they must have written them to suit Anna's case.

By the time I heard the result of the hearing two weeks later it was 3½ years since Anna had left me under the sheet. Although I had long got over the sheet work itself, I hadn't got over losing Anna. But I wouldn't have been true to myself if I had tried to keep quiet about it. My trust in her was completely lost any way.

Anna's training organisation found her to be in breach of eight points of their code of ethics - half the total points on their list. They placed a number of sanctions against her that have actually had the effect of finishing her career because they are too expensive for her to adhere to.

---

[1] Sukey Montford, Advocacy Support Worker
[2] John Mackessy, Advocacy Support Worker

Rather than even trying to adhere to the sanctions, Anna announced her early retirement and as a result her organisation struck her off.

I went back to see Pat just once, after the hearing, to tell her about it. She was clearly quite ill and told me that she had cancer. A short time later she wrote and told me that she was giving up work altogether, permanently. This left me with further issues and so I started seeing another counsellor shortly before Christmas 2004. I am no longer seeing her regularly. I think I have issues too deep for her to deal with and I don't know what the answer is now.

The story doesn't end there because Anna appealed against the findings of the hearing. Unbelievably one of the things in her appeal was that she was protesting that she knew the member of her organisation who was Chair of the hearing board. If it had gone in her favour would she have been making a fuss about that then? Before the hearing both her and I were asked if we knew anybody on the hearing board and she must have said no. Presumably she must have thought it helped her case that she did know her.

She lost her appeal and then tried to appeal through the UKCP.

Then in summer 2005 POPAN rang and told me that Anna's membership of the UKCP had lapsed some years previously! POPAN sent me their copy of Anna's submission for the UKCP appeal. At the time I could only face having a quick look at it because it angered me so much to see what Anna was saying about me when I had no chance to respond to it. When I eventually got round to looking at it – all 200 pages of it, I wrote to Anna telling her about the bits I strongly objected to. For instance she said that I had written to the BBC complaining about her, which was utter rubbish. She also said it had always been my intention to finish her career. How could she say that when my attachment to her had been so strong? I never did want to end her career although I have no regrets that this has since happened.

It didn't look as if Anna could appeal through the UKCP after all but last spring the UKCP decided that they could hear Anna's appeal against her organisation's handling of my complaint. Can you believe it? This was going to take place last November but it was postponed and is due to happen some time early this year I believe. The date has not yet been re-set.

I still haven't got over it all and I don't know if I ever can. I invested so

Broken Boundaries

much in Anna both emotionally and financially. I had the best relationship with Anna that I had ever had with another female in my life. My attachment to her was really strong and some of my feelings towards her still remain. I have never really wanted to make trouble for her and yet I needed some resolution to what happened. That attachment was intensified by her lack of boundaries in many areas quite apart from her hugging/holding me. I now believe that if a therapist/counsellor has physical contact with a client then they need to have very firm and clear boundaries in other aspects of the relationship. Anna was more like a friend than a therapist in many ways but I trusted that she knew how to handle everything - including the ending of my therapy. Although I did have anxieties about this, when I discussed these with her she was always so very reassuring. Of course neither of us could have foreseen just how bad the ending was going to be for me.

It was like I was abandoned by Anna on the day of the sheet work, 9th April 2001 and like she left me there then and never came back for me. My trust in her, and others, has been completely destroyed. Losing her was the worst part. In many ways it seemed like I was emotionally back where I was in the past before I started therapy.

I thought Anna really understood me like no one else ever had done. Something was seriously wrong with her understanding of me for her to leave me under the sheet - because it so closely repeated the way I had been treated by the bullies at school who ran off and leave me alone in the park during games of hide and seek. Anna knew all about that and so how could she put me back in so similar a situation? It has never made sense. Did she in fact ever really understand me at all?

My aim in having therapy was so that I would be able to mix with people and make friends more easily. Although I am better at actually making conversation than I was I know that I still come across to others as if I am aloof and anxious to get away from them as quickly as possible. My experience has made this worse and I believe I fear attachment to people. I used to believe that I was too needy and might come to depend upon someone too much or simply put people off because they could see my neediness. Since my experience with Anna, I am also scared of being misunderstood. How can anyone else understand me if I could be so misunderstood by a therapist to whom I had spent so many hours talking? I talked to her more than any body else in my life. If she could miss me so completely and hurt me so much what could other people do to me who don't claim to have my interests at heart? It seems to me that my progress has been stunted and crushed by what happened.

Judith Field

I believe I was very badly wounded and that this was all extremely damaging for me. I had been so attached to Anna for so long and I really thought she could help me overcome all my difficulties. I believe I trusted her more than I have ever trusted any other woman in my life. It seems like I was dreadfully betrayed and abandoned by the one person whom I thought was going to help me recover from everything. What happened with Anna dwarfs everything else in my past.

Although Anna never has apologised to me it did help that the hearing was in my favour. I don't regret anything that I have done.

5

Sarah Richardson

Anyone can become angry, that is easy; but to be angry with the right person, to the right degree, at the right time, for the right purpose and in the right way - that is not easy.

Aristotle

I was in my last year of Junior school when the abuse started. Aged thirty-seven, it still haunts me.

I was asked to write about my experience with my mental health worker, which is how I became acquainted with WITNESS when the case was taken up by the General Social Care Council (GSCC, the regulatory body for social workers). I felt that if I were to tell my story, I needed to tell my earlier history in order to benefit the potential reader. I need to do this both in terms of the power of words as a healing tool (for writer and reader alike) and, because my abusers were both in the medical/caring profession. I hope to highlight that perhaps, our institution of NHS care needs to root out those whose sole purpose of 'care', is to abuse and potentially destroy their victim's lives. I also feel that abusers assist in the destruction of the very meaning of that common used word 'care'. It is my hope that recounting my story will encourage others, in whatever capacity, to have the courage to speak-out. We all have a right to be heard and to be listened to, even if that was denied to us at the time. I must stress however, that listening alone is simply not good enough. We must all constantly work towards eliminating these individuals who abuse their position of 'care'.

My mother's boyfriend was a paediatric nurse at the local general hospital.

I was around ten years old when he attacked me. I use the word 'attacked' as opposed to word 'raped' as my mind has blanked out the finer details of what he actually did do to me that night. I am just left with a huge gaping void and whether that will ever be revealed to me (in whatever shape of form that may be) I do not know. What I do know is that he entered the darkened bedroom and closed the door, and the next person I saw was my mother stood at her dressing table. She asked how I was, to which I replied "it hurts down below". (Actually, it more than 'hurt' it felt as if I had been ripped open inside). To which my mother passed me a tube of KY jelly and said that this should help. As she left the room and turned off the light I lay in the bed tapping the light switch above my head, absolutely and terrifyingly numb with shock. I recall vividly the feeling of my ten-year-old mind totally unable to grasp the reality of what had happened when this man had visited me. In fact, I actually felt it switch onto standby mode. I have never been able to access, clearly, and with 100% certainty, the missing parts of my memory. I feel very angry that, whereas some people or person may know the details of that night, I do not. I so want my mind returned to me intact, as it was on that night before I entered my mother's bed. It is an anger that lies dormant inside me, but still I can feel it sometimes, deep inside me, twisting and turning around like a snake buried within my stomach.

Because the relationship my mother had with the paediatrician was clandestine, my mother claims this man was not allowed to form any sort of relationship with either myself, or my elder sisters, nor was he allowed to see us. I find this hard to believe. Unless my own mind deceives me, I remember having several conversations with him, in person and on the telephone, along with a number of accidental meetings, all instigated by him and always alone, throughout the years he was sharing a 'friendship' with my mother. The night the attack happened I was ill with the mumps and was resting in my mother's bed. I was unable to sleep, as my head pounded with fever, and loud music. The music that rose up to me was from one of my mother's 'Newly Found Freedom' parties (in her new home) that she hosted, after separating from my father.

I will never be able to comprehend that night just as I fail to comprehend my mother's answer to my statement. So, for the next 25 years I said no more about that night, not to my parents, not to anyone. In a desperate attempt to gain answers to what had actually happened to me, and more importantly to try and regain the pieces to my memory that seemingly would not give up the ghost and allow me to access it, I finally did break my silence about what happened that night. My mother's only comment on the matter, years later, was that I was ill, it most certainly did not happen and that a childhood fever could produce a state of delirious night dreams that originate from an overactive imagination. In basic terms I made it up, therefore it deserves and has continued to deserve, no further comment.

Part Two

Stephen Thompson came into my life at a very traumatic time for me. After gaining a degree and a teaching qualification, I had a very brief counselling period (my first in thirty-four years.) alongside coping with my first 'full time' lecturing post. This was also combined with a personal relationship that was becoming more and more volatile as time went on. The result of these pressures on me was, simply put, to crash and burn out. I just could not see a way forward for me as the stress was taking a huge toll, and my mental health began to significantly deteriorate. I had reached a point in my life where I could no longer cope with my past, nor my future, so I ended up taking an overdose. My partner (at the time) took the decision not to take me to the hospital but rather to the doctors, days later. My blood tests proved negative and luckily, I had sustained no long term damage to my health. However, he did instruct a mental health social worker to make an appointment to visit me. Unfortunately, the social worker put in place neither set a structure, or proposed care-plan, so I felt completely in the dark about what this man was supposed to be doing to 'care' for my mental well being.

After the initial appointment with my social worker (at his office) he began to visit me on a weekly basis at home. I tried to keep the earlier, conversational, appointments very brief. I felt uncomfortable revealing to a complete stranger, who I had yet to learn to trust, the true extent of the state of my mental health. As a single mother of three children, I felt very guarded about revealing what was going on inside my head . . . was he a spy? Would my children be removed from my care if I confessed to my suicidal and self-harming tendencies? I could not answer, nor rationalise these fears for myself and did not want to confess such fears to someone whose job and purpose were never explained to me; so the fear and isolation continued, physically and mentally.

I regret now that I had not trusted my initial instincts more, as from the first conversation I had with Mr Thompson I felt a negative vibe. I had explained that my counsellor had thought that I had body dysmorphia, to which he replied, "Well, clearly you have a lovely figure". (The essential feature of Body Dysmorphic Disorder (BDD) is a preoccupation with a defect in appearance. The defect is either imagined, or, if a slight physical anomaly is present, the individual's concern is markedly excessive. DSM-IV 1994) Feeling very unnerved, I pushed these negative thoughts from my mind and went along with whatever he recommended as beneficial to my treatment. After all, he was the professional in charge of my mental health care, who was I to question his methods?

It was only after 3 or 4 visits that the physical contact started. I was brought up to believe that when people visited your home, it was polite, upon their departure to show them to the door. And this would be the precise moment that he would put his arms around me for a goodbye hug. I felt extremely uncomfortable; in fact I hated it, feared it, even. I could not understand why he was doing this, putting me into such an awkward and powerless position. Powerless is exactly how I felt. All of my instinctive emotions were screaming inside my head 'this is wrong, this is just not right, this just should not be happening to me'. Surely, I have a right to my own personal space and for that not to be abused in any shape or form. Hours later, after he left, the anger at myself for having such an inability to prevent this uncomfortable situation occurring, would begin to feed at my gut. Why couldn't I just push him away and say assertively "I do not like this"? The only thing I could do to ease the mental anguish that this situation caused was to drown it with alcohol and drugs (some prescribed, more often and finances allowing, non-prescribed). After all, the feeling of numbness and disembodiment was something I had learned early in life as a coping mechanism, regardless of the consequences that my actions may have upon my mental and physical health.

So the debate inside my head as to whether or not I should be hugged and cuddled continued. At the time I was in a professional career myself and was working primarily with vulnerable youths. I questioned myself and answered with logic. I would under no circumstances engage in bodily contact with my students. If they presented themselves under extreme distress I would, possibly, place my hand upon their shoulder, but always with another member of staff in the room. However, I was unable to put this view into practice with regards to my own care and my debating mind continued. Maybe he felt sorry for me and wanted to show he cared for me and that he cared about what happened to me. His visits often coincided with my 'bad days', and these were the days that he would hold me tighter and for longer. I once confided in a friend of mine but she dismissed my fears and told me that he was only showing me that he cared. I felt bad for my earlier thoughts and reprimanded myself severely for seeing a caring touch as something with potential sexual intent. It was at this point that I began to have some terrifying flashbacks, in dream form, to my earlier experience. If, like my mother, my own friend supported the view that I see platonic gesture as something more sordid and sexual, then maybe it was all just 'in my head' and I was the one at fault. Was there something I was doing unconsciously to encourage this? I concluded that, yes, it must be me.

Intuition is a powerful force and one should never dismiss it. How can we ever learn to protect our own self, our own body and mind, if we don't trust the warning signals they give us? I still struggle to believe that I found it more acceptable to trust someone I hardly knew, and other's comments, rather than what my own mind was telling me. Regretfully, the hugging continued and I just learned to accept it, get used to it even, however uncomfortable I felt inside. I must admit that this situation only added to the utter hatred that I felt for myself, the fact that I did nothing to stop it. Preferring to hurt my own feelings rather than upset his by telling him that "Yes I did have a problem with being cuddled, a bloody huge problem in fact", as he did ask me once, with arms wide open, if I minded. I really thought that I did not need to answer the question as my body language spoke volumes where my muted tongue failed me. I was wrong.

As the visits continued and time went on, my mental health rather than beginning to improve, deteriorated, and I tried once again to overdose. This time Mr Thompson took me to the hospital to be checked out and stayed with me throughout the duration of my stay. I was sent home with no detrimental affects to my health, apart from the rising anger that welled inside because I could not even succeed at exterminating myself. After this happened I began to learn to trust my 'carer' more and more. Maybe he did really care about my well-being, after all he brought me gifts of CD's; accompanied me to the finance office when I could no longer afford to keep up with my payments; collected my prescriptions from the doctors; made telephone calls to my place of work to confirm the state of my ill-health, and better still he increased my dosage of antidepressants, without me even having to go to an outpatients appointment! I came to rely upon his care and learned to trust him and what he had to say when we had our weekly discussions, which included my returning to work. He felt I would not be able to cope with returning to such a demanding position, (although he never expressed this so explicitly), and I listened intently as he talked about when he gave up his teaching position. I cannot say categorically that our discussions resulted directly in my decision to terminate my full-time employment with the local college, however, this is what happened. On the 1st September 2004 my resignation was accepted and my employment in a career that I had studied so hard to achieve for the last four years, ended. I felt a total failure and worse still I had severed any contact that I had with the outside world. I felt isolated and alone, sinking deeper and deeper into the quagmire of depression. The only light on the horizon was, I felt, that I still had the help and guidance from my social worker.

His life, past and present, dominated our conversations... wasn't this meant to be about how I was feeling/coping etc? I seemed unimportant to our weekly conversational meetings. He made frequent references to my libido and how depression affects it that seemed to have no bearing to me. I once again dismissed the uncomfortable feelings that this evoked and tried to change the subject. He once told me that I should be very careful in my choice of partner as I attracted people who would abuse me. I decided that if this was the case, and why shouldn't I buy into that theory with my past history, I would refrain from forming any sort of relationships with friends or otherwise. One can never be too cautious. It appeared to me, upon writing this testimony, that the pinnacle of Mr Thompson's abuse of his position, happened when I was at my most visibly distressed. Maybe, if Mr Thompson's theory is correct, that I do indeed attract abusers, something unconscious encouraged his despicable behaviour towards me. However, I most certainly think not!

My state of mind, at the time, had reached a pinnacle. It was summer season and now logically I can understand why there were so many flies about, both inside and outside the house. However, in my anxious state I was unable to be logical about such things. I had decided that due to the flies, there must be something rotting in the home. As I could find nothing after having scrubbed and scrubbed the entire house until my hands were sore, my mind concluded that what was actually rotting was my own body. I felt that I could smell the rot seeping out of me and that the flies wanted to lay their offspring within my decaying insides. The night before Mr Thompson's visit I had one of my many disturbing dreams. I had dreamt that I was a child and that people were trying to talk to me, but I was too embarrassed to talk to them, as I had a massive penis growing out of my mouth. The penis began to grow larger and I started to choke. As the people around me became persistent to involve me in their conversation I began to cry and tried desperately to cover my mouth so that they wouldn't see this thing sticking out of me.

When Mr Thompson arrived I tried to discuss the reasons for my fretful state. He said of my dream that I should have bitten off the penis and made a gesture towards his genital area and said "Ouch!" I did not discuss my dream any further as I felt he was turning what was extremely traumatic for me, into a joke. He remarked once again about depression and libido and gazed around the room asking why I had so many pictures of semi-nude women. I felt it was a very crude way of looking at the works of art of Picasso and Schiele and this made me feel very uncomfortable as I wasn't sure where this vein of conversation was leading. At this point my mobile phone rang, which frightened me, as the moment it went off a fly buzzed passed me. I began to cry. I do not like anyone witnessing my distress and I immediately felt embarrassed so I made excuses that I had an appointment, and I then followed him out to open the door for him, he immediately put his arms around and held me very tightly. As I always did, I kept my arms very still next to the sides of my body, in the hope that my body language would suggest that I did not like this. He released his arms and touched my nose with his finger, which seemed to me a rather romantic gesture and I began to feel very apprehensive at what he was going to do to me. He held me again, tighter this time and said "I know what you need is to be taken to bed, but I'm afraid that is out of my jurisdiction". He continued to hold onto me as if waiting for an answer. As he pressed against me, again, I could feel his erection. I broke lose from his arms and opened the door. He checked on the next appointment and then left. Feeling absolutely numb inside I locked the door, went upstairs, took several sedatives, curled up in my bed and cried.

I eventually confessed what had happened to my Psychotherapist, but swore her to secrecy. She showed no surprise that this had happened as she had had certain reservations herself about Mr Thompson's involvement in my care. A week later I visited my GP I asked him to stop any further visits from Mr Thompson and revealed the reason that I came to the decision. I had to work up a lot of courage to do this as I still thought that if I did not have these visits then my children would be taken away from me. I was informed at a later date that my children were never considered to be at risk and that this was not the reason for Mr Thompson visiting me at home. Although this was a relief to know, it didn't make up for all the months of worry this misconception had caused me. My doctor explained to me that as this was such a serious matter, he would have to report it. He made a telephone call as I sat next to him in the surgery. A sudden fear washed over me, what if I had got this all wrong? It did not seem a serious matter to me, and I wondered if I had maybe made far too much out of it. I severely regretted the decision to reveal the details of what had happened with Mr Thompson. I felt for a long time that I was being ungrateful for all the things that Mr. Thompson had done for me. And I felt terribly sad for his family who would, undoubtedly, be very upset.

North Lincolnshire Council completed an internal investigation and as they didn't find enough evidence to substantiate the claims that I made against Mr Thompson, the matter was dropped. No formal letter was ever sent to me explaining the outcome of this investigation despite the fact that they had visited me twice in my home in order to obtain a statement. I was later to find out, at the trial brought against Mr Thompson by the GSCC, that Mr Thompson had been reprimanded by his previous employers for inappropriate physical contact with a vulnerable female client. It came out in the trial that the previous employers did not think that the incident would be repeated and therefore this was not taken any further. I find it hard to believe, after hearing that particular evidence, that North Lincolnshire Council dismissed the complaint (when it was first made) against Mr Thompson for insufficient evidence! The stench of a cover-up congests my nostrils too much to think about the lack the 'care' that Mr Thompson's employers have shown me, as regards his second offence. His second offence I say in terms of what has been reported, as no one can quantify those who cannot, for whatever reasons, stick with their complaint or even make the initial complaint.

I conclude this testimony with the facts up to date, as regards Mr Thompson, who still practises to this day as a Mental Health Social Worker.

I was requested to attend a hearing (as a witness) brought against Mr Thompson by the GSCC on Tuesday 30th January 2007 at 9.15am. The facts that were admitted by Mr Thompson and therefore found proven by the Conduct Committee were:

(1) In 2004, Mr Thompson had inappropriate physical contact with service user Miss A by putting his arms around her on one occasion;

(2) During 2004/2005, Mr Thompson had inappropriate physical contact

with service user Miss B (myself), by hugging her on several occasions;

(3) Mr Thompson did not prepare a written care plan for service user, Miss B (myself).

The Committee found Mr Thompson guilty of misconduct and directed that the appropriate sanction in this case was to place a record of admonishment on Mr Thompson's registration for the maximum period of five years. Unfortunately, the case was not strong enough to uphold the full allegations that I gave evidence on. Although, I have been reassured that this does not mean that I was not believed, it is still hard for me to conceive, that the only facts that he has been found guilty of are those that he admitted. More importantly, the GSCC chose to take the easier option, by dismissing the sexual element of the allegations as 'not proven.' Do they themselves struggle to recognise and acknowledge that perpetrators of 'sexual' abuse in the employment sector, are possibly being given sanctuary by the General Social Care Council by their inability to prove these facts? Are the GSCC in some way colluding with the perpetrator when they go with the safer option, the less uncomfortable option, the cleaner more sanitized option, because it is easier to prove in a legal sense? I must stress that I am very grateful for the fact that The General Social Care Council brought the case before the Conduct Committee, however I feel that there is still much to be learned if these cases are to be successful. After all, the very least that the victim of abuse deserves is justice for what has happened to them.

It was explained to me, upon several occasions, that the case against Mr Thompson WAS strong enough. That is the very reason why I decided to put myself through the trauma of recounting such deeply personal details to a room full of strangers. I wanted justice. I got a whitewash. I believe that the sacrosanct GSCC must adopt a zero-tolerance policy of sexual abuse by social workers. They could do this, or at least make a start, by doing whatever it takes to ensure that allegations of a sexual nature are upheld, rather than taking the easier option just to ensure that they get some result. The GSCC could have handled this better by explaining the problematic legal procedure to me beforehand and listening to my views and opinions on the matter. After all, I was the one that the abuse happened to; I am the one that this has affected; I am the one whose direction they should have taken into account. All that they have achieved, in my case, is to perpetrate the disempowerment of ME, the victim. I am not just one of many, Miss B's, I am not just a name on a statement, I am Sarah Richardson, I have a voice and I want to be heard. I do not want to take the easy option and had they have listened before the trial they would have heard that. Maybe it was 'easier' for them not to hear.

The GSCC have a choice to make here whereas I and many, many others have been denied a choice. And, whilst they can go home at the end of their working days feeling confident that they got, at least in part, a (safe) result, and understandably, forgetting the days' events, I am denied that safe haven of forgetting.

6

Jo Adams

In May 2003 after some dreadful life events, I became very depressed. My G.P prescribed antidepressants, which made me feel considerably worse. I was in an uncontrollable downward spiral and after weeks of trying different tablets, there was little or no progress. I had to push myself to go to work and each day became harder. In June I started to feel that things were unreal and that everything was moving in slow motion. I told my husband that I did not know how I could continue, and took sick leave.

I began feeling very scared and had terrifying panic attacks. I never had trouble sleeping, but on waking my heart pounded and I wondered how I would survive the day. I was also extremely agitated, particularly during the mornings. If I woke early I would force myself to go for a run. My suicidal thoughts scared me; and I was petrified of being alone in the house for fear of what I might do to myself. I was very self critical, believing that I was totally useless. My interest and concentration levels were poor. It seemed everyone else had worth, while I did not. It was a truly terrible time. When my mother couldn't be with me, she would telephone hourly to check how I was and reassure me.

Broken Boundaries

The three months I had off work were mostly a blur. Barely able to look after myself let alone my family, I went to live with my parents for a while. Everyone told me the more time I had off work the harder it would be to return. In September, trying to get some normality in my life, I went back to work, despite feeling extremely embarrassed by my medical condition. By October there was no improvement. So I went back to my GP. He referred me to Robert who was the surgery's part time counsellor. It seemed pointless as I truly believed there was nothing or nobody that could get me out of my hell. But I reluctantly agreed, thinking he could do no harm.

I saw Robert for six fortnightly sessions. He gave me homework to do, for example, making a note of everyone who was nice to me before the next session. I noted that a bus driver had let me on the bus without payment. To this he put his hand to his mouth and whispered, "I bet he fancied you". He asked to see my childhood photos; and we talked at length about my relationship with my mother. He said I should cut the apron strings and be more independent and assertive. As a result of this I had a huge argument with her and we fell out.

He paid me compliments, made me laugh and he self disclosed. I can clearly remember him telling me that he needed to lose weight. He also told me about the most embarrassing moment in his life. There were other conversations we had, although I no longer remember the details. As I left my final session, Robert said, "I hope you don't mind me saying, but you are pretty". I walked out of his room feeling quite confident, more so than I had in a long time. I thought he was the answer to my prayers so I wrote thanking him.

He replied saying:

"As far as writing to me goes, please continue!! I do really want to know how things are going. At present I still feel rather like your counsellor and am happy to be so, perhaps given time that relationship may become friends, however that offer has to come from you. Ethically. I can't suggest it".

So we continued corresponding.

I then received my first phone call from him, asking how I was. He said he was leaving work, had no more clients that day, and had nothing else planned. On hindsight, I wondered if he was hinting that he was free to meet me. And it seemed odd that he should call me.

Soon after, Robert phoned again. We talked about my welfare and chatted. Later that day, I noticed he was parked outside my house. Shortly, he drove away but 5 minutes later returned knocking on my door. I invited him in for coffee and we had a normal conversation. Then suddenly he said "Do you realise, I'm a member of BASRT[1] and can't have sex with you for a year." I did not understand what he meant. He then said he was a member of another organisation, whereby it was OK to have sex with an ex-client after 6 months. He was smiling, so I thought he was joking, and I laughed. When handing him coffee, my hands shook and I nearly spilt it. The whole visit made me very nervous and disorientated, although I enjoyed his company.

Robert started visiting me regularly, sometimes as often as four times a day. I felt flattered and more confident with his attention and soon started feeling affectionate towards him.

He visited me most often on Tuesdays and Fridays, his surgery days. The other weekdays he worked at a community hospital some miles away. He nevertheless frequently made excuses to be with me, which I found very complimentary. Sometimes when Robert came round, he said that a client had cancelled. He should have telephoned the next client on the list, but hadn't. One day after a huge argument with my mother, I was terribly upset. He chanced to phone whilst she was still with me and arrived minutes later. I had to introduce them to each other. Later when we were alone he said he had cancelled his next appointment as I had sounded upset and he was very concerned.

I could not stop obsessively thinking about him and did not understand my feelings. He was 18 years older than me, had greasy hair, smelt unpleasantly of body odour and had a long unkempt beard. I never found him physically attractive. In all ways he was the exact opposite to my much-loved husband. As well as writing secretly, we began texting. Some of his texts became very sexually explicit. Although I was embarrassed I also enjoyed his attentions.

Robert then asked me to meet him for a drink, and I suggested we meet in the city. I subsequently told my husband about this, but Robert didn't tell his wife. He talked about mostly personal and family things, in particular that his wife didn't satisfy his sexual needs. When we got outside he gave me a small teddy bear. Afterwards I had very mixed feelings, the evening had been enjoyable, but I felt guilty and my mind was a jumble.

---

[1] British Association of Sexual and Relationship Therapy

Broken Boundaries

I found myself thinking about Robert more and more, and before long felt I couldn't live without him. My depression lifted considerably, I was often elated now instead. He encouraged a family friendship, as his two daughters were a similar age to mine. Several times, Robert, his wife and children, my husband, myself and our children all went out on family days together.

One day Robert drove me to the coast. Neither of us wanted to return as we were enjoying being together. Back in his car, he asked me to kiss him, and I did. On the way home he stopped in a lay-by and we talked about our relationship. Afterward I felt excitement, tremendous guilt and self-hatred and fear of my dependency on Robert. Although I told him that we should just be friends, I felt totally hooked on him. Even though I told him about my confused emotions, and fears of depression, he still encouraged my dependency. By then he was visiting constantly and one day asked me to sit next to him on the sofa and we started kissing. I can remember thinking, "What the hell am I doing?" I pulled away and cried. He said it was just a bit of fun and nothing to worry about. He agreed we should just be friends but added "friends who kiss". I couldn't face my husband when he returned from work, so as soon as he got in I went for a bike ride. I felt torn between my wonderful husband and him. My emotions were so intense; I thought I had lost control. Always my fears of depression kept me from ending my relationship with Robert; and I went along with kissing, hugging and holding hands mainly through my fear of losing him.

One day Robert said I would make an excellent counsellor and that sitting in on some of his sessions would build my confidence and give me good experience. He even said we could go into partnership together and encouraged me to start a counselling course immediately. Subsequently, he saw two clients at my house and I sat in on these sessions, having been introduced as his colleague. I felt most uncomfortable and embarrassed, particularly as one was an acquaintance of mine.

For his birthday I bought Robert a counselling book that I knew he wanted. For my birthday, he bought me some underwear. Two days later, when he visited, he asked me to put them on. I refused but he was insistent. Out of fear, I went upstairs to comply but covered myself with a dressing gown. When I came back downstairs, he was undressed, and then tried to make love to me. Reluctantly I kissed and cuddled with him, but refused to go further. Again I couldn't face my husband, and went straight out on my bike just after he arrived home.

I continued punishing myself both mentally and physically about what had happened. It was too much to bear and I hated myself. He said his marriage was on the rocks and he wanted to leave his wife and family for me. He said that he loved me but didn't love his wife. Countless times I tried to end our relationship but was always scared of going back to the hellish depression I was in before. He told me more and more about his private life, I often felt he was using me as a counsellor. He also discussed patients at the surgery, some of whom I knew. Despite my reservations Robert constantly talked about sex and told me the most intimate details about his home life. He frequently compared his wife unfavourably to me, and at times I felt quite sorry for him.

I felt on a real high at times, but also felt torn in two and very distressed, there were too many emotions to deal with. Robert insisted I no longer needed my antidepressant tablets, so I stopped taking them. I felt alone and unable to tell anyone the complete truth about my situation.

Eventually I realised that for the sake of my mental health I had to stop seeing him. Again I was slipping back into depression but this time over Robert and all my unwanted feelings. But when I tried ending things entirely, he lied and was very manipulative. He had always been possessive and controlling, but now it got worse. For example, he told me I wore too much make-up and that he didn't like me going out with girl friends. His insistence upon still visiting and calling, made me realise that his motives were not solely to help me. When I texted to say I could take no more, he replied saying, "Please don't stop the hugs and kisses I need them and I need you"

He would not leave me alone, he knew all my movements, and would follow me in his car to and from the bus stop and school. One day I got to work and broke down in tears. As I was in no fit state to work, I was sent home. On the way home I rang my husband and told him everything. I then called Robert and told him what I had done. His first words were, "That's me fucked". Robert phoned my husband that evening and said that his feelings were too strong and that he couldn't help himself. He pleaded with my husband not to tell anyone. As I was in such pain and feeling so ashamed, I too asked my husband not to report him. Robert and I then agreed not to see each other anymore. The next morning when I awoke, my husband was staring at the ceiling with tears streaming down his face. In 20 years I had never before seen him cry. I had never even considered being unfaithful before either. I cried continuously. Although I tried to keep it from my daughters, they knew I was very sad; and they were very reluctant to leave my side. We had to explain some of what happened. It is not just the victim who suffers but their families and friends as well. But at the time, I didn't even realise that I was a victim.

Still he did not leave me alone but continued following me in his car, and trying to speak to me. He said that his wife blamed me equally, adding that since his wife had found out about us their sex life had improved. I replied "I didn't come to you to make your sex life better". He admitted he had done wrong, and said that a day would not pass without him thinking of me and how he enjoyed the times we shared together. I just stood there and sobbed.

One morning I knew I needed help. My head was spinning, it was hard to breathe and I shook uncontrollably. I walked to my GP's surgery and said, "Please help me". I had no intention of reporting Robert then but when the doctor asked if more counselling would help, I sobbed and almost screamed. I told her everything. She put her head in her hands, shook her head and said "No". She then said that they already had reservations about him and called my own doctor in. They both said that they believed me. I was immediately put back on my medication and given a sedative. They asked if I had anyone who could look after me. My mother would have been the obvious person but I had fallen out with her because of Robert's advice. They sent a Community Psychiatric Nurse (CPN) round but I kept falling asleep during his visit, due to the sedative.

Two days later I had a meeting with the Surgery's Practice Manager. She said nothing could be done because the 'so called' affair took place post counselling. She was obnoxious. I got the impression she wanted to sweep this under the carpet. She said she would have to make enquiries and get back to me. But her attitude changed completely in subsequent meetings. Within a week Robert lost his job both at the surgery and at the community hospital.

My depression was the worst it had ever been, I feared it would never improve. My thoughts were totally irrational and although my CPN called weekly, I was getting steadily worse. On his advice, I found another therapist, a lovely lady who was horrified at what had happened. After a while, with her help and support I reported Robert to his governing body. But as I was still making little personal progress, my GP referred me to a psychiatrist who sent me to a Cognitive Behavioural Therapist as well. I called Witness who provided advocacy and tremendous support. They also gave me the name of a very good solicitor, should I wish to take matters further. After speaking to him, and a lot of soul searching, I decided to instigate legal proceedings against Robert. I have never regretted my actions. At this time I still blamed myself and hoped the legal process would persuade me that I was not to blame. This has indeed been the case.

It has now been nearly three years since we last had contact. I am still on medication, although it has been reduced. Life has been incredibly difficult at times, but I have become a lot stronger. A very good friend of mine said, "Living well is the best form of revenge" How true I have found this saying.

I thought I was alone in experiencing both this type of abuse, and the feelings that followed. But I'm not. During the past two years, I have heard many other survivors' experiences. All people, like me, who were vulnerable and in desperate need of help, not further harm. Different stories, but remarkably similar feelings and emotions, with a range of triggers for reliving it all. My worst ones are songs of the time, especially The Closest Thing To Crazy by Katie Melua, hugely evocative of my feelings then. Hearing it even now can still sometimes reduce me to tears. It is not only during daytime that the feelings still come back. I have terrifying nightmares even now, filled with fears of returning to deep depression and worthlessness.

Along the way I've been in contact with some wonderful people, some so special that we have become very close friends. It has been so helpful to speak with others who have been through similar experiences. There have been many positives, and I now have a confidence that I have never had before.

7

Melanie Cunningham

Dr Morgan presented himself as a caring man when I went to him as a new patient in a depressed, traumatised state. I was fighting to overcome my battered state, but childhood abuse, tragedy and extreme cruelty by my ex-husband had overwhelmed my life. I had small children and I was alone with no family support.

Following a prolonged custody battle, during which my ex-partner launched a smear campaign against me attacking my mental health from all angles (including a betrayal by my mother), I was finally awarded custody of the children. Despite the constant character assassinations by my family, the legal psychiatric reports were good, stating that I was a good mother.

After several months of 'grooming' (which I had no knowledge of then) the doctor started sexually abusing me in my home, under the guise of counselling.

I was in a state of shock, unable to stop what was happening – this man with such power – a pillar of the community. It was hard to believe that my trusted GP could be doing such an evil thing to me when I was in such a vulnerable state. Doctor Morgan knew my tragic history. He also had full knowledge of my struggles to secure custody of the children. He learned of the terrible pain inflicted on me by their father, the legal process and the relatives who had elevated themselves to amateur shrinks. He knew of my continuing fear that my ex-husband was just waiting for 'evidence' he could use to reverse custody.

At my request, Dr Morgan made a referral for my children and I to get counselling at the local hospital. The sessions were unhelpful though – I felt 'observed' rather than counselled, as the process linked us to a social worker.

Dr Morgan abused me in my home for two years. Naturally, I became increasingly distressed as I suffered this nightmare in secret. I felt violated, bathing each time, weeping from torment, trying to wash Dr Morgan off my body. He would abuse me when the children were away from the house, either at school, nursery or with their dad on an access visit.

As the horror worsened, I struggled to maintain my daily routine and even became suicidal for a brief period. The children were always my top priority and I was afraid about the future. My fears were confirmed one day when the hospital social workers asked me to voluntarily put them in care. They said it was due to my 'distress.' I was terrified as I now faced losing my children to them and my ex-husband.

Both options were devastating. This caused me to feel an acute sense of powerlessness and as though I was trapped. I refused their suggestion.

Summer approached. My ex-husband was due to have the children for a few weeks as agreed. The children had places at school for the autumn term. My youngest was about to begin her infant class while my eldest was to join primary school.

Before they left, I received a very clumsy phone call from a junior social worker. She enquired whether I was giving custody to their father. I told her I was not; and she terminated the call. The entire topic had been clipped short as if a spurned salesman was beating a hasty retreat.

When my children were due back from their visit, their father telephoned me and said that he would not be returning them to me as the social workers had blackmailed him. He told me that the social worker had threatened to take the children into care if he brought them back to me.

Despite my urgent visit to the police and the fact that he was the non-custodial parent, the children remained there with him.

Dr Morgan wormed his way into the legal quagmire that surrounded the custody case of my children. He condemned the social workers' malpractice and assured me that he would defend me in court. He penned an affidavit in which he supported me having custody.

Throughout the legal chaos, Dr Morgan abused me with stealth, even though I had now lost my children. My shock and grief increased tenfold because of it. I became aware that this was an abuse of power, but reporting him was impossible. He had become my primary legal witness and I could not jeopardise this second custody case.

I was angry, though, at what he was doing, and accused him of abuse. It was then that he changed into sadistic, cunning aggressor. He blackmailed me with threats of whether or not he would help me in court as it loomed nearer. Previously he had boasted how he would 'roar like a lion' in my defence.

Over a year later, my husband was granted full-custody by default, after the legal teams forced me into an out-of-court settlement. My protests about the miscarriage of justice were silenced with more blackmail. Doctor Morgan broke his promise to me and took no action. The roaring lion had mutated into a fleeing mouse.

In retrospect, it was a vital opportunity for Dr Morgan to maintain my silence. It felt like some sort of 'gentleman's arrangement' about which I will never know the truth. In the end, Dr Morgan agreed to oversee the implementation of the court order for 'staying access.' My children never came home.

In the 1990's I reported Dr Morgan to the General Medical Council (GMC). I was put through a lengthy filtering process before I got to the final hearing. My case was backed by the Community Health Council (who told the GMC that it was a serious case of sexual abuse) as well as POPAN (which is now called WITNESS). I turned over copies of several years worth of personal diary entries to the GMC. They included all of the dates on which Doctor Morgan abused me. The solicitors dissected my medical records looking for 'dirt.'

I underwent an independent psychiatric assessment as requested by the GMC. The report was positive, concluding that my report of abuse could not be psychiatric based. The medical defence's main argument was a massive attack on my mental state. My personality was crushed from all angles. The defence said that my allegations were 'fantasy and nonsense.'

The GMC hearing lasted for two nightmarish weeks. The focus was not on his so-called 'professional misconduct' but on an in-depth examination of my mental condition and medical history. The line of questioning by the defence was ferocious. They spun verbal circles round my entire life, which included personal betrayals by people I trusted. I felt like a criminal rather than the victim of a scavenging, manipulative doctor.

The intimate details that I provided for the GMC as evidence included: the year of Doctor Morgan's vasectomy, his fear of impotence, lack of circumcision, a description of his underwear and an unusual garment tied over his vest. They used a poem that I wrote about the abuse along with some pants that I gave him as legal exhibits. The Panel however, accepted the defense's explanation for my knowledge of Dr Morgan's vasectomy; that it was 'common knowledge.' As for the strange garment; I could have seen it in the laundrette.

The GMC never suspended Doctor Morgan, pending the inquiry. No expert witnesses were called on behalf of the prosecution. There was no appeal facility. The psychiatrist subpoenaed to the GMC court was never called to the witness stand. The GMC legal team represented both myself and the GMC simultaneously.

The press covered the GMC case against Doctor Morgan. The coverage was supportive of me up until the end when Doctor Morgan was acquitted due to 'insufficient evidence.' Once he was found not guilty, I was described as a liar. This added to my pain and outrage.

Today, I am coping with complex post-traumatic stress-disorder as a result of these shocking experiences. I lost my children, my professional career, my home and my family because of Dr Morgan's abuse.

The situation with my adult children is not yet resolved. At present, they are missing from my life and I am heartbroken. I hope they will learn the truth one day about the events that spiralled beyond our control. I believe that love is stronger than corruption, abuse or injustice.

Doctor Morgan once said, 'Truth will win in the end.' Ironically, this reality could ensnare him spiritually or otherwise.

About This Book

Broken Boundaries grew out of a project that was grant-funded by Awards for All. WITNESS wrote to everyone on our newsletter mailing list and asked people who had first hand experience of professional abuse whether they would be interested in participating in our project. We ended up with five women who were able to write their stories and join us on a day facilitated by Lorraine Millard. The women each wrote a first draft, which I read through and did an initial edit prior to the workshop.

We discussed with the women what they might find most helpful and they decided that they would like to hear each other's stories. We gave the participants a choice of whether they would like to read out their own story or to have Lorraine or I read it out. Some of the group members were reluctant to read their own stories at first, but by the end everyone had decided to do so. The participants said that it was incredibly powerful to read their stories out loud and they found it particularly moving to hear the stories of other women. Two women contributed their stories separately after the workshop. The stories all went through an edit cycle involving WITNESS staff and an external professional editor until they arrived at their final form.

Lynn Hiltz
WITNESS Services Manager
April 2008

About WITNESS

WITNESS is a small charity providing a range of specialist services. Resources for victims and survivors include online and offline information products, a helpline and support services. WITNESS also provides training and education about professional boundaries and works for changes in policy law and practice. WITNESS relies on donations and sales of products for its income.

Our website is www.professionalboundaries.org.uk

We are grateful for comment and discussion about this book and this can be done through info@professionalboundaries.org.uk. We can also pass on communications to the authors.

Selected Further Reading

For people interested in further exploring writings on boundaries and boundary violations the books below have been selected as a primer. All are currently in print and easily available; information about more books is available by contacting WITNESS.

Fish in a Barrel. Grace Tower. Millennial Mind Publishing 2005
One of the most recent published personal accounts. Lots of interest and much here to learn about how manipulated therapy clients can be when the need to trust and believe in the professional is strong. Grace Tower's story encompasses both the abuse and her own journey through various proceedings. This is a no holds barred account of a damaging abuse committed by a highly controlling perpetrator.

Shouldn't I be Feeling Better by Now? Yvonne Bates (Ed.) Palgrave 2006
Excellent up to date personal accounts by therapy clients. Many stories of serious abuse of both the boundary violating and transferential kinds.

Sexual Abuse by Health Professionals. S Penfold. University of Toronto Press 1998
Sue Penfold is both psychiatrist and survivor of professional abuse. This book details her experiences and is an invaluable source of information about the dynamics of professional abuse.

Boundaries and Boundary Violations in Psychoanalysis. Glen O. Gabbard, Eva P. Lester. American Psychiatric Publishing 1995
This book includes a fascinating history of early boundary violations amongst the founders of psychoanalysis. There is also much on transference, gender, supervision, institutional responses and clear accounts of sexual and non-sexual violations in psychoanalysis.

Psychotherapists' Sexual Involvement with Clients - Intervention and Prevention. Gary Richard Schoener et al. Walk-In Counseling Center 1989
A comprehensive guide to abuses by helping professionals: history; prevalence; therapeutic responses; groups; advocacy; law; treatment; prevention; supervision and a great deal more.